"Values are like fingerprints.
You leave them all over everything you do."

—ELVIS PRESLEY

"Valuegraphics takes the ol' time religion of demographics and stands it on its head. Better yet, this book delivers an effective and essential replacement."

— **Don Peppers and Martha Rogers, PhD, co-authors of business bestsellers, including *Managing Customer Relationships and Experiences: A Strategic Framework*, the definitive textbook in the CRM and customer experience field**

"It freaks me out that David maybe knows me better than I know myself, and his gin martini vs. vodka martini case study turned my world upside down. James Bond, take note."

— **Douglas Coupland, designer, visual artist, and author of thirteen novels**

"The practice of demographically defining audiences is so well established that it is easy to forget that it comes with a hidden cost: it may often be a self-limiting belief—a constraint on your thinking and on your creativity. Valuegraphics by contrast is liberating—since it helps provide us with a why and a how to complement the who."

— **Rory Sutherland, Vice Chairman at Ogilvy Group, author of *Alchemy: The Surprising Power of Ideas That Don't Make Sense***

"We've known for a long time that values reveal crucial consumer insights. Finally, we have a data-based metric to back it up. This is a global game changer."

— **Dorion Carroll, VP of Customer Engagement Technologies at Amazon**

"People everywhere are making decisions based on their values. This book couldn't be timelier. It explains what's happening right before our eyes. As a lifelong marketer, I believe a successful brand or campaign is based on connecting with your customer in a meaningful way. This approach guarantees we will get it right."

— **Christine L. Delucchi, SVP of Global Marketing and Communications at Hines**

"If you don't read this book, don't even *dream* of calling yourself a marketer. David has turned everything we know about predicting consumer behavior right on its pretty little, backward, antiquated head. Your first response will be: What the hell have I been wasting my time on? And then the lightbulb will shine brighter than it ever has before."

— **Kate Bradley Chernis, Co-founder and CEO of LatelyAI**

"I've always been confused about demographics—how come I'm more millennial when I'm apparently a Gen X? And then I came across Valuegraphics, and it all made sense. It's not about when we were born—it's about the values that drive us. Once you understand this, you see the world, your team, and clients in a whole new way, and you suddenly understand exactly how to motivate them. All those Gen Z and millennial experts out there: consider yourself on notice! This book proves that nobody acts their age anymore."

— **Carina Bauer, CEO of IMEX Group**

"Consumers do not make decisions based on their demographics. So why do we use demographics to try to understand consumers? David Allison cuts through the noise, outlining concrete strategies you can take to unleash a more accurate and profitable marketing and engagement strategy rather than relying on outdated and inaccurate demographic profiling. Refreshing, insightful, and thought-provoking, this book is packed with colorful case studies that will ensure you never look at your consumers the same way again. A must-read for anyone in the marketing world."

— **Shane Feldman, serial entrepreneur, keynote speaker, and television personality**

"This book is a must-read for every customer-centric business leader. It examines how any company can gain an unparalleled level of customer insight and the competitive advantage that goes with understanding customers' true motivators: their values."

**—Ginger Conlon,
Thought Leadership Director at Genesys**

"As someone who studies human behavior for a living, I rely on Valuegraphics to help me more effectively understand people and why they do what they do."

—Seth Mattison, founder of Futuresight Labs, international speaker, author, and business performance advisor

"Mindful marketers align with their audiences by incorporating data, creativity, and purpose. David's new book brilliantly touches on all three areas. It's essential for making wise product and marketing investments. Obsessions with demographics bring bad karma to well-intended growth plans!"

**—Lisa Nirell, CMO adviser, podcast host, and author of
*The Mindful Marketer***

For Christopher the golden-hearted.
Because he is the best thing
that has ever happened to me.

THE DEATH OF
DEMOGRAPHICS

DAVID ALLISON

With a Foreword by Don Peppers and Martha Rogers, PhD

THE DEATH OF
DEMOGRAPHICS

Valuegraphic Marketing for a Values-Driven World

Copyright © 2022 David Allison

All rights reserved.

The Death of Demographics

Valuegraphic Marketing for a Values-Driven World

ISBN 978-1-5445-3461-9 Hardcover

978-1-5445-3462-6 Paperback

978-1-5445-3463-3 Ebook

CONTENTS

PART FOUR
THE DIY VALUEGRAPHICS TOOLKIT

PART FIVE
THE 15 VALUEGRAPHICS ARCHETYPES

FIVE-MINUTE VERSION OF THIS BOOK

First off, thank you!

Each time someone buys a copy of this book, it proves to me that there are other people out there just like me—people who want to live in a values-driven world.

But maybe reading this book, at least right now, is too much to handle? That's fine. I get it. Life is hectic!

Or maybe you are the kind of person who likes to have a quick overview before you dive deep into a topic? I see you. I'm the same way.

That's why I made a five-minute video that covers the key talking points from this book. Just go to **www.valuegraphicsbook.com** and it's yours for the asking.

SOME HINTS

by Don Peppers and
Martha Rogers, PhD

WHAT HAS DAVID ALLISON
ACCOMPLISHED HERE?

WHEN WE WROTE OUR FIRST BOOK IN 1993, BEFORE THE
internet was in widespread use, we thought we were on to
something. We felt driven—no, compelled—to write a book,
and combined with our speaking engagements, this kept us
busy enough to prevent our assaulting civilians on the street,
grabbing their lapels, and having to tell them about (what
was then) the future of business, based on emerging radical
changes in technology (including the World Wide Web).

Clearly, David has the same passion for the work
he started in 2015. He wants to save you from making

mistakes, from losing out competitively, from missing the Understanding Data boat. He couldn't *not* write this book. Aside from helping with the success of your business, it will also help us understand how detrimental stereotypes can be and how we build a better culture and commonwealth because of it.

In a nutshell, he has taken the ol' time religion of demographics and stood it on its head. We've all openly or secretly suspected for decades now that age, income, education level, marital status, and the like were not the best way to plan communications strategies. But they are all so easy to measure and to use to define people and somehow project their possible needs. Maybe. What David offers us now is not just a way to elevate our strategic thinking about customers and how to reach them and communicate with them effectively. He is also a persuasive storyteller and arms the reader with examples that make the Valuegraphics Database—in all its global and mathematical glory—easy to understand and talk about.

Once you understand Valuegraphics, you will need everybody you work with to get it, too. If you are trying to reach customers, you want the media companies you use to offer this as a way for you to find and direct messages to your audience. If you can choose between a television station or online magazine that can only sell you women ages 18-35 in the northwest part of the country and one that tells you how you can buy people of any age who value family, creativity, and environment because those are their core values, then which will you buy? Demographics? Or Valuegraphics? Which will lead you to better success?

HOW TO USE THIS BOOK

There are six sections in this book.

Part One tells us where we have been and why that won't work anymore. It's like a brief history of Rand McNally maps compared to your most effective GPS. Read every word of this section. No skimming. This will make you a better conversationalist at parties and will underpin your argument later when you have to do battle with the demographers.

Part Two tells us where we are going and why. It delves into behavioral science and helps us understand how we can use psychology, sociology, and neuroscience in a scientific way to do what we all want to do: to convince people to do something that is in their best interests. It describes the birth of the Valuegraphics Database, as well as its basic methodology. And the complete list of the fifty-six values that run your life. Read every bit of this too, and take the time to work your way through the list. This is not work. It is power. Don't skip over any just because they are not valuable to *you*. If it's on this list, it's valuable to somebody, and you may need to connect to that somebody. You may be trying to do it now.

Part Three tells us how different parts of the world are different based on the values of the people who live there. By learning more about the values of other regions, you will learn more about the values within your more relevant regions. You will become proficient in a wide range of values that help you to put the most important first. (You will also become better at understanding the BBC world news reports, and that will make you smarter at making decisions, too.)

You will be tempted to read only the sections where you know people, where you have customers now, or where you like to travel. *Don't*. This is not your horoscope. Read it all, or you will miss important insights about the values that are important to people outside your own worldview. And read it all to get a full understanding of the values, period. Even if your audience is contained entirely in one local county or even one country, you will still profit from reading it all. And you'll enjoy it.

Part Four is an insight into how to understand the archetypes revealed by the global database. In most regions, one or a few archetypes dominate the population. This helps us understand how to select the short list of values that are more motivating for, let's say, our Workaholic customers than for everybody else. And how using them, which David calls "our North Star values," to make decisions will ensure we are magnetic to our customers. You guessed it. Do. Not. Skim. Why would you rush through the section that reveals what to do with the values that describe your audience and prospects? Or how to make the most of what you've learned?

Part Five, handily, is an overview of the fifteen Valuegraphics archetypes and comes with its own instructions, so all we will say is: don't miss it.

Part Six is two appendices. The first provides you with a set of compelling case studies, told the way Aesop would tell a wise fable but with illustrative business results. You don't *have* to read this section unless you want to cement what you've already learned so you can start being fluent. Besides, you will have the most fun in this section because these are all true stories. Maybe yours is next. The second appendix is a glossary of terms you will soon not be able to live without.

WHY DOES IT MATTER?

Now that the Valuegraphics Database has worldwide coverage and the archetypes and definitions have become more familiar and easier to understand, the next frontier is not just knowing what but understanding *why*. And then follow-on strategy becomes that essential frontier.

A mass marketer's traditional method of operating used to portray each product as distinctly different from other products but then treat every customer the same, appealing to all of them at once with the same basic brand message.

Because of the new technologies now available to remember and interact with customers individually, however, it has become relatively easy and inexpensive for a company to *treat different customers differently*, one customer at a time, and it can do this in a cost-efficient way even if there are millions of customers. Importantly, however, the same new technologies that now allow all businesses to remember their customers from interaction to interaction, and to treat different customers differently, have also empowered customers themselves. With the click of a mouse or a tap on a phone screen, today's customer can get instant access to information about a brand or a product, and the source of that information is no longer limited to the brand's own advertisements or commercial messages. In the process, customers have become less patient with and more demanding of the businesses they deal with.

They can interact instantly and conveniently with their friends, business colleagues, and family members via a host of different channels, from voice and text to websites and mobile apps, and guess what. They expect to be able to interact instantly and conveniently with the businesses they patronize as well. And they *expect* every business they interact with to remember their interaction the next time so that they don't have to tell a business the same thing over and over.

In other words, while businesses have been doing their best to adapt their marketing strategies to adjust to this new reality, customers themselves have begun to demand that companies also adapt their sales, customer service, and customer support activities. The result is that every company's marketing, sales, service, and support functions—virtually the whole customer-facing side of their operation—have been smashed together into a single business activity that centers around the "customer experience."

Moreover, the deeper and richer any customer's relationship's context becomes, the more competitively defensible it will be. For a business, a deep and rich context to its relationship with an individual customer is like an "economic moat," protecting it from its competitors with respect to that individual customer's patronage. We call such a context-rich customer relationship a "Learning Relationship" because the business is constantly learning more and more about the individual customer's needs and desires. The online bill-pay customer is engaged in a Learning Relationship with the bank; the more payee names and addresses the customer enters into her bill-pay app, the more the bank itself learns about how to satisfy her own individual needs, quickly and conveniently, and the more a customer benefits by not switching to a new bank and having to start all over.

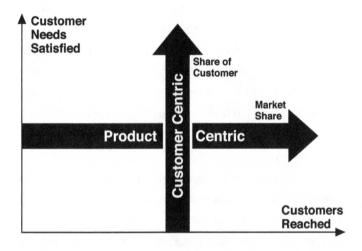

The traditional, product-centric competitor focuses on one product at a time—a product that meets some widely held customer need—and tries to sell that product to as many customers as possible. The customer-centric competitor focuses on one customer at a time and tries to satisfy as many of that customer's different needs as possible—across all the company's divisions and business units, and through time as well (i.e., meeting a customer's needs week after week, month after month). And while the product-centric competitor measures success in terms of market share, the customer-centric competitor measures success in terms of its share of customer, with respect to each individual customer.

Importantly, the vertical direction of our two-dimensional marketing space is not defined by the products a business makes or sells but by the different customer *needs* that it can meet. So when we think about "share of customer," we shouldn't think just in terms of wallet share. Rather, we need to ask ourselves what share of this customer's needs are we meeting? What share of the customer's *life* are we participating in? And what additional products or services might allow us to increase our participation in the customer's life overall? Said another way, while a product-centric marketer's goal is to find more customers for its products, a customer-centric marketer's goal is to *find more products for its customers*.

Customers are no longer segments of a population who have something in common that doesn't matter to *them* and only matters to marketers because it's easy to define. Instead, customers and audiences are looking for someone to do business with who "gets" them. Someone they can trust to understand what they need, when, and how, and to remember them and treat them differently based on this deep and always-learning insight. The same holds true for prospects—the customers we haven't met yet. It's why we must understand, respond to, and lead with our customers' core human values. *Each* customer's core human values.

It means reducing the *friction* in the system, the transactions, and the relationships. It's why we work together with our customers. In our parlance, it means becoming more trustable. Higher trustability results in higher customer profit for a company and is based on doing things right, doing the right thing, and being proactive. It's not so much that customers love to say they value "trust" in a company, but when they do trust a company, they believe the company understands them at their core, looks out for their best interests, doesn't create hassles, and is proactive. Each of these elements will work more effectively when the company is speaking to the deepest foundation of a customer's beliefs and tenets.

The Valuegraphics Database, and the strategy that led to the careful and extensive scientific protocol that delivers it, provides a leg up in improving customer relationships and increasing the financial value of a customer to a company through a better understanding of the values that drive the customer. Further, it means using the customer values that create company profits in a way that makes it easier and easier for a customer to do more business with your company.

ORGANIZATIONS HAVE, FOR THE LAST DECADE OR SO, BEEN collecting incredible amounts of customer data. Because data is gold. Data is safe. Having data to support decisions makes us look smart.

As a result of our prolonged data binge, we now know the most granular details about our target audiences. Every blink, bounce, like, click, and step is recorded and made into a chart. But we have been ignoring the most enormous elephant in the boardroom.

Data doesn't cover the last mile.

The "last mile" is a term that describes the leap between *having* all the data and *using* it to make decisions. How do you make data actionable? What will you do next? No matter how much data we collect on a target audience, the decision about *what to do about it* is left to guesswork and intuition.

It's like being a chef. You can study at the greatest cooking schools in the world. You can learn about the lives and techniques of the most respected chefs. You can know more about sauces, spices, and seasonings than anyone ever has. But when it comes time to attract patrons to your restaurant, you must still use guesswork and intuition to design a menu and hope the decisions you make lead to a bustling dining room. If you guessed wrong, you try again. And again.

Eventually, hopefully, you'll find out what customers are craving, and your restaurant will be the busiest place in town.

Companies around the world collectively spend trillions of dollars each year trying to engage target audiences. Anything that reduces the risk of their last-mile decisions could potentially save billions of dollars. If they knew in advance *exactly what their target audience wanted*, they could focus on giving them that and not worry about anything else.

And herein lies the problem. Marketing teams around the world have been using demographics—and to a lesser extent, psychographics—to determine what their audience wants. Demographics determine who we are, they imagine, and so they collect and arrange the data into demographic profiles. But those profiles don't actually tell you who people are and how they behave. Not even close. Because there's only one thing that determines what people do, and that's their core values.

Our core human values are the driving force behind every decision we make. They determine what we choose and why and how we behave. This is the proven scientific truth behind valuegraphics—a new way of looking at people based on what they care about. What valuegraphics offer is that elusive solution all companies seek: bringing new certainty to that last mile.

WHAT THIS BOOK IS ABOUT

This book will show you how to understand valuegraphics and harness their potential. I'll share some well-studied but little-known secrets from various fields of behavioral science. I'll show you the results of an ongoing global project that we've been working on for years, which led to the creation of the Valuegraphics Database. And I'll give you a simple set of tools that you can use to understand what your target audience cares about and what they value most of all. Moreover, I'll give you a DIY process to implement your learnings so you can use the information in this book now, immediately, to make things happen.

- Marketers will learn how to connect the dots between products/services/brands and what their target audience wants. We shouldn't waste precious resources talking about what we think is important. We should talk to our customers about what *they* think is important. This book will show you how.

- Creators of all kinds will see which core human values will lead to the most captivating products, services, brands, CX, UX, and more. Once you know what your target audience cares about, you simply give them as much of that as possible, using everything you have at your disposal.

- Embracing valuegraphics also has a super-nice side effect for everyone involved. Your organization can unite around a set of values as a magnetic North Star to guide everything you do. Driving toward a destination derived from data is a great way to end frustrating friction or polarizing politics. Anyone who has ever engaged in a battle to ensure a great idea wins the day will know exactly what I am talking about. Valuegraphics are a squabble reducer and a power leveler. And who doesn't want that?

At the end of the book, I've added an appendix of *case stories*—a light version of *case studies*—about how valuegraphic data has worked in different situations and places. I chose specific stories that will, hopefully, help you see how valuegraphics work in the real world and the impact they can have.

BETTER MARKETING AND A BETTER WORLD

I remember breaking into tears during an interview with a journalist from France. We were in an elegant cocktail bar in Manhattan, holding icy martinis. He kept asking why I was doing what I do.

I started to explain how we built the Valuegraphics Database to make philosophical behavioral science ideas into empirical data, but before I could finish, he shook his head.

"That's not my question," he interrupted. "Why are you doing this? Why is it important?"

I tried another angle. "Ageism is a by-product of demographics," I explained. "So is sexism, racism, homophobia, classism..." I was trying to show how demographics force us to create assumptions about people that lead to harmful stereotypes. To progress as a world, we needed to discard our systemic reliance on demographic stereotypes.

He pushed me further. "Yes, but you still have not told me why *you* are doing this."

I switched off my journalist-answering autopilot, and I took another swig of my martini. I paused for an awkwardly long moment to consider what he was asking. And instead of answering with my brain, I spoke from my heart.

I told him how I felt about our fractured and divided planet and how desperately we needed to find solutions. As I did, I felt a lump forming in my throat. I pointed out how harmful and hurtful demographic stereotypes were, and I started to tear up. I listed example after example of demographically fueled hatred and conflict. I was weeping now and—not kidding—had to ask him to hold my drink.

That was the first time I said all of this out loud. It was the first time I acknowledged how this work aligned with my values and my belief that we can change the world if we change the way we look at the world. That, to me, is the core of the Valuegraphics Project. We get to talk to people about what they care about, understand them based on what they value, and begin to see the world as it really is. This is our moment to abandon demographic stereotypes and look at each other based on what we have in common, the core values that make us human.

That martini moment was roughly five years ago. Since then, more and more organizations are embracing the bottom-line benefits of valuegraphics. I am asked to speak all over the world. Universities and textbook companies are including valuegraphics in marketing coursework. All these positive steps reaffirm that we can make this change in the world, which makes me even more determined to disrupt demographic stereotypes.

And that's why I wrote this book: to teach more people

how to harness the power of shared human values. I want to give marketers and creators an alternative to antiquated demographic profiling methodologies from days gone by. This is the best way I know to help the world get to a better place in a better way: by helping everyone use what we've learned so far and by continuing to share whatever we learn in the years ahead.

PART ONE

THIS IS WHAT WE'VE BEEN DOING WRONG

CHAPTER I

MY BIGGEST
MISTAKE

UNTIL 2015, I OWNED A MARKETING AND CREATIVE SERVICES firm that specialized in a unique kind of work. Our clients were high-end real estate developers building condominium towers, resorts, and sometimes entire communities. Our work was in Canada, Europe, the Middle East, the United States, South America, and the Caribbean.

Every project we worked on began with a target audience brief, meant to answer the question, "Who are we building this for?" It was our job to take that information and create the most compelling and motivating marketing campaign possible, designed to sell, lease, or rent hundreds of millions of dollars' worth of real estate.

Truth is, those target audience briefs were mostly inter-changeable. My clients were always convinced they were building for the same people—baby boomers. Wealthy baby boomers, of course—the ones who had all the money. To help us understand the particular subset of wealthy baby boomers they had in mind for a new project, someone would whip up a profile or persona, and it would generally read something like this:

MEET BOB & SALLY

Bob & Sally are baby boomers who live in the suburbs and are on the verge of retirement. They live in a nice house. They renovated the kitchen last year and also installed a media room in the basement. They paid off the mortgage five years ago, after decades of hard work and sacrifice. With the kids gone, it is time to sell the house, use some of the money to buy a maintenance-free condominium to live in for part of the year, and spend the rest of their time in a warmer climate. They love Costa Rica and hope to have enough money to buy a small second home there so they can put down roots.

Bob has finally stepped down from his executive vice president role at Associated Enterprises. And Sally has started to tell her piano students that the lessons in her living room will soon be ending. Both are looking forward to having more free time to relax and spend time on their hobbies. Bob has a woodworking shop in the garage, and Sally loves to sew.

Bob drives an entry-level C-class Mercedes. He has always wanted to have a Mercedes. Finally having one makes him feel like all those years of working long hours and saving his money to pay off the mortgage were worth it. He spends Saturday mornings washing and polishing his car in the driveway in front of their home. The Mercedes is his pride and joy.

Sally can't wait for her turn to indulge. In the new condominium, she wants an enormous closet because she loves clothes. Not expensive clothes necessarily, but she likes to stay up to date with the latest fashions and that means "freshening up" her wardrobe on a regular basis. They'd never had enough room for a walk-in closet or enough money for Sally to fully give in to her love for shopping, but she hopes that after they sell the house, that will change.

These Bob & Sally stories could go on like this for page after page. They were filled with demographically induced assumptions based on gender, age, income, number of kids, education level, and career achievements. There would also be psychographic information about favorite brands, activities, interests, and what Bob & Sally wanted from a new home in terms of amenities, features, and price.

I saw so many Bob & Sally stories. I wish I had saved them. They would have made a fascinating book—a snapshot of a moment in time when we all assumed wealthy, baby boomer, empty nesters like Bob & Sally were an interchangeable mass of buyers.

My company would use a Bob & Sally story as a guide to develop a campaign strategy. Then we made billboards, websites, elaborate sales centers, brochures, advertisements, social posts, contests, radio commercials, and so on. We made everything as appealing to Bob & Sally as possible so that they would fall in love with these condominiums and buy one.

We were good at this work. As a result, 99% of the time our real estate developer clients would sell out quite quickly. Two or three years later, the tower would be ready for people to move in, and there would be a welcoming party, a ribbon cutting, or a press event. It was a great chance for us to see all the people who our campaign had attracted. And the most curious thing happened over and over again.

Bob & Sally didn't show up.

We'd be at those events looking around, holding a glass of wine in one hand and a prawn skewer in the other. There would always be one or two Bob & Sally couples milling around, but they were the odd ones out. Instead, there were all kinds of other people from all walks of life. Bob & Ted couples in matching cardigans. Busy professionals checking their Apple watches for incoming text messages. Wide-eyed folks from out of town who'd just bought the second home they'd been saving for. Too many varieties of people to list! Who were all these other people, and why had they shown up when we hadn't targeted them? Where were all the other Bob & Sally buyers we had spent so much money trying to engage and influence?

It was a mystery at the time. But today, we understand why Bob & Sally didn't show up in the numbers we had expected. They didn't show up because *people who resemble each other demographically have almost nothing in common*. It's impossible to create a message—or a product, service, or brand, for that matter—that will appeal to an entire demographic target audience. We've done an enormous body of research that backs this up, which we'll explore in the next chapter. But first, let's look at why demographics have been so important to us throughout the ages and why they no longer work.

A BRIEF HISTORY OF DEMOGRAPHICS

Demographics are older than language. Demographic stereotypes were the rules and expectations that kept society together. To ignore them was a serious infraction of the social code and could result in the extinction of your bloodline. Your demographics were your destiny, and it was serious stuff.

Let's start with a Flintstones-era description of a demographically defined life.

If you were a young man, it was your job to hunt and kill giant snakes for the delicious snake patties your mother was famous for making. People came from all over for those grilled snake patties with a side of steamed river grass and a cup of fermented goat butter tea.

You also had to be prepared at a moment's notice to grab your spear and skewer your enemies, who were always creeping up to the morning bonfire, trying to steal pots of food or precious tools. From time to time, you were also expected to bludgeon and stab the inhabitants of a neighboring region in an all-out war, so there was always that to look forward to.

However, if you were a young woman, you had a different job: making babies. The more babies you produced and tended, the better chance your village had of growing and surviving thanks to the fresh crop of hunters, warriors, and baby makers filling in the ranks behind the current batch. In your downtime, you cooked and made clothes.

Older women and men were the respected elders.

They didn't have to do what the young men and women did because they were old. They would sit around being wise or painting ceremonial pictures on rocks.

Fast-forward a few thousand years, and we are transported to a middle-class suburb in the United States in the 1950s. What's going on around us now?

After a complex and ritualistic initiation ceremony that lasts four years, referred to as an undergraduate degree, young men have a specific job to do. Every morning, they put on their ceremonial armor (suits and ties) and leave the cave (the bungalow) to hunt and gather and provide for their family (earn a paycheck). The successful ones become vice presidents, and a few are so good at hunting and gathering that they are asked to lead all the others in the role of chief.

The chief, better known as the chief executive officer or CEO, is handsomely rewarded. He is given the use of elaborate rooms in which to sit and think (offices), commune with other chiefs (private clubs), and make decisions (boardrooms). He wears regalia to communicate power and prestige, perhaps a Rolex watch, Italian leather shoes, and a custom-made suit.

The women stay home to bring up the kids, cook the meals, and clean the house. They gather with other women from time to time to exchange stories and knit sweaters and mittens. They swap tips on how to get the kids to fall asleep faster, make ground beef into a tasty treat with a few simple spices, and use plastic armrest covers to keep the sofa looking as good as new.

Obviously, I'm hyperbolizing. But not by much. Demographics, throughout history, have dictated what was required of you at certain times of your life, based on your gender, marital status, number of kids, occupational category, and the like. Demographics were, in fact, a complex system of stereotypes and expectations set down for the greater good to ensure the survival of the species, or at least of your particular tribe, village, corporation, or community.

You can see how demographics helped us survive in the Flintstone era and how, as time went on, these social codes became ingrained and then restrictive. Demographics put you in a box. They determine what is expected of you throughout your life to help your society function. There was a time that if you were born in a village in northern France and you weren't having babies by the time you were 14 years old, you faced a penalty. If you were a young man born in the plains of Africa, and if by the age of 13 you weren't carrying a spear and hunting, then you were not pulling your weight. There were penalties to pay for not being married, not producing children, not working—in other words, not doing your part. And it was all demographically defined. Old people had a job; rich people had a job; poor people had a job. There were those who rebelled, of course, and did as they pleased. But depending on where and when they decided to let their freak flag fly, those aberrant behaviors attracted swift retribution. In some places and times in history, you might simply suffer from social shaming. At others, you could have your head chopped off and hoisted up on a stake as a warning to others who dared express themselves differently. Coloring outside the lines was never a good idea.

WHY DEMOGRAPHICS ENDURE

Apart from the survival of the human race, there's another reason for the longevity of demographic labels and the stereotypes they create. I'm referring to heuristic thinking. Here's a great definition:

> "A heuristic is a mental shortcut that allows people to solve problems and make judgments quickly and efficiently. These rule-of-thumb strategies shorten decision-making time and allow people to function without constantly stopping to think about their next course of action."[1]

Imagine this. You are on a nice post-lunch walk through the desert after a double helping of stewed dates and soft cheese, your favorite comfort food. You are looking up at the sun, which seems particularly large and angry today, when you spot a tiny row of dots on the horizon line, far off in the distance.

You squint at the dots and realize they are rapidly growing larger. Soon, it becomes clear why. Those dots are actually a dozen young men on horseback wearing red headgear and blue robes that you do not recognize, and the horses are galloping directly toward you. There are no women, children, or elders among them. They are clearly heading for the oasis where your tents are set up, where your family and friends are lolling about digesting the midday meal.

You turn around and run back in the direction of your encampment. As you approach, some of the others look up, curious why you are moving so fast after eating such a large meal. The sun is in the exact right position to block their

---

1 Kendra Cherry, "What Are Heuristics?" Verywell Mind, February 13, 2022, https://www.verywellmind.com/what-is-a-heuristic-2795235

view of the men on horseback gaining ground in the distance behind you, so they are oblivious to what's going on. Finally, you are within earshot and you yell at the top of your lungs. What did you say?

Now imagine this. It's the day of the 1967 Consolidated Enterprises Annual General Meeting in a suburb outside the city of Chicago. It's been held in the same hotel ballroom with peach-and-brass stackable chairs and matching table skirting for as long as anyone can remember. It's the only place in the area that can hold all the managers and senior staff who travel in from the satellite offices and serve everyone a proper sit-down meal afterward, too.

The proceedings never vary. Dressed in gray suits, the chief executive officer and other C-suite executives file out on stage. They take their places behind a long table and take turns reading ceremonial statements. From time to time, a vote is called, and with no dissension, the gavel falls and another motion passes. It's been this way for decades—for as long as anyone can remember.

This year, however, while everyone is milling around outside the ballroom waiting for the proceedings to begin, you notice something out of the ordinary.

By your count, there are 27 people off to one side who are not wearing gray suits. They have longer hair, even the men, many of whom also have beards. The women are wearing denim cutoffs or billowy skirts, and some are barefoot. They seem quite agitated and are talking loudly among themselves. An occasional outburst of laughter drowns out the din, after which the chattering returns.

You slink past the crowd, slide into the ballroom as

covertly as possible, and make a beeline for the senior secretary. She knows where the CEO is sequestered with the rest of the C-suite executives. You give her a message to pass along, and you tell her to hurry.

What did you say?

You know precisely how you'd react to the men on horseback galloping toward your napping tribe. Without even stopping to think about it, you would make a snap judgment, leap heuristically to the conclusion that a bad thing was about to happen, and run back to warn the others to grab their swords and prepare to slice up the intruders. Your brain used demographic observations to leap to a conclusion that would save the lives of the ones you love.

And you know exactly what you'd tell the secretary to say to the CEO in the peach-and-brass ballroom. There were protesters in the lobby getting ready to bust into the room and disrupt the orderly agenda. You used demographics to leap to a conclusion about people and take decisive action.

Our brain uses demographics to make snap decisions and to cut down the amount of time we have to think about something. Simply put, it saves us time and energy—it's a heuristic shortcut. The problem is, that shortcut can be extremely limiting, both for how we understand the world and how we react to it. It's based on stereotypes.

LET'S TALK ABOUT PSYCHOGRAPHICS

Although a much smaller field than demographics, psychographics also plays a role in how we understand the world.

Psychographics, like demographics, are a way of profiling a group of people and trying to understand who they are and what they are all about. A Google search for "definition of psychographics" displays 121,000 results. Myself, I like to think about psychographics simply as "a record of past behaviors and emotions."

Psychographic data is collected in a myriad of ways, and new methods seem to pop up every week. We monitor the location of our customers with geo-tracking on their phones. We conduct brand-emotion studies to find out how loved or hated a company is. We map the clicks on a website to see how to maximize the customer journey for the next visit. I've lost track of all the innovations around psychographic data because frankly, it all comes from exactly the same place—the past. It shows us what's happened so far. It doesn't help us with the last mile. It shows us patterns that we could possibly take advantage of if we wanted those behaviors to continue, but that's about it. It doesn't help us understand how to change those behaviors and convince people to do something different than what they'd done before.

When I'm on a stage delivering a keynote, I'll sometimes pick out a member of the audience in the front row and explain psychographics something like this:

I want to talk for a moment about my friend here in the front row in the red sweater. What's your name? Doris? OK. Hello, Doris. Thanks for being here today. Now, Doris, I'm going out on a limb with this, but I'm going to guess a psychographic fact about you is that you drink at least three cups of coffee a day. Correct? OK, good. This is a record of how Doris has behaved in the coffee category so far. Now, if I was in the caffeine business,

I'd love to know that Doris drinks three cups of coffee a day because that helps me understand her current behavior. However, it does not help me understand how to get Doris to drink six cups of coffee a day, or change brands of coffee, or try cold brew coffee instead of what she drinks now. It doesn't tell me how to get Doris to consider tea, or maybe even switch to Red Bull for her caffeine fix in the morning. Psychographics are useful to a point, but just like demographics, they do not tell us what we really want to know: how to bridge the last mile and minimize the guesswork required.

DEMOGRAPHICS TODAY

Today, rigid demographic expectations and social norms have largely fallen away. In many parts of the world, for example, children don't have to start earning a living at 12 or 13 years old to ensure their family and community survives. Not *everywhere*, of course—there are still huge inequalities around the world. In many countries, people *do* need to work at 13 years old to keep their family afloat, and other demographic battles remain to be won. But it's undeniable that we've made progress from, say, the 14th century, and that we're closer to being truly free to live our best lives than ever before.

What *will* get us to that finish line? Discarding demographic thinking. We need to stop using demographics as a way to look at the world. Demographics create stereotypes that cause divisiveness and strife. Homophobia, ageism, sexism, racism, classism—these are enormous social problems that come from looking at people with a demographic lens, the way our ancestors did. We're not going to rid the world of these issues unless we get rid of the demographic stereotypes that fuel them. And that starts with reframing how we think about the world and each other.

It won't be easy. Demographics helped us survive and evolve and was the basis for an exceedingly complex web of sociocultural norms that defined every aspect of our lives. Moving beyond them will be slow work, but it is possible.

How does this apply to marketing and businesses? Should we get rid of demographics altogether? My answer is no. Demographics *are* useful, but we've been using them for the wrong things. We've been using them to profile a group of people and say, *Now that we have their demographics, we understand who they are.* But we don't—we simply understand *what* they are. And there's no link between what people are and what they'll do next.

Think of it this way. If you have a room full of middle-aged women who earn $100,000 a year and have a college degree, then all you can truly surmise about them is that they're middle-aged women who earn $100,000 a year and have a college degree. That does not mean they're going to be similar to each other in any other way at all. You know nothing about their emotions or their likes and dislikes. You don't know what drives them. But companies have been using demographics to describe *who* people are and what they'll do next, which has led to stereotypes that we now use to define target audiences and run our businesses. And that causes all sorts of harm.

Demographics are the Dewey Decimal System of humanity: a great way to organize people into groups based on similar outward-facing characteristics but not an indication of what those people are all about on the inside. In a library, the Dewey Decimal System is the wayfinding tool that tells us we will find historical fiction in aisle six, on the third shelf from the top. But assuming all works of historical fiction are the same is clearly ridiculous.

BOB & SALLY—AGAIN

Wait a minute, you say. If demographic thinking doesn't work, how did you sell those condos to a room full of people? The marketing was a success, wasn't it? The Bob & Sally profiles worked!

No, they didn't. Remember I said how in that room full of people, only one or two couples resembled the Bob & Sally target audience description and that everyone else was completely different? Well, it turns out everyone in the room was incredibly similar after all. We were just looking at them in the wrong way. The people who showed up and bought those condos had something far more powerful in common than age, income, number of kids, or any other demographic label in the target audience description. They shared a set of values, and they bought the condos because they saw their values reflected in our messaging.

We didn't know we were using the power of shared human values to attract buyers for our clients. It was a happy accident. If you spend enough money to spray-gun enough messages in enough channels, you will eventually attract the attention of enough people who share a set of motivating values. *Marketing as we practice it today relies on accidental impact.*

In retrospect, it all seems horribly inefficient. But at the time, it was all we knew. Back then, I assumed—as we all did—that demographics could define a group of people who were similar in meaningful ways. We thought demographics gave us the insights we needed to persuade people to do something. But if we step back and look at this assumption of demographic similarity, it quickly falls apart.

We're not simply claiming this based on the Bob & Sally story. We have statistically accurate research to prove it— more than three-quarters of a million surveys from around the world, executed with the help of a team of translators who speak 152 languages. If you want data-backed proof that demographic stereotypes are not your friend, the next chapter should do the trick quite nicely.

CHAPTER 2

DISRUPTING DEMOGRAPHICS

SOMETIME BEFORE 2015, I BEGAN WONDERING IF demographics really were the best way for companies to engage and activate their target audiences or if there was a more effective way. Remember, demographics are useful for putting people in categories, but they are terrible at explaining who they are and why they behave the way they do. And the same is true for psychographics: they are a great way to record what people have done so far, but they don't tell you how to impact what they will do next.

That's why we launched the Valuegraphics Project. We wanted to create an inventory of core human values and give organizations values-driven target audience profiles. I'll go into more detail about how we collected the data and built the Valuegraphics Database in Part Two, which is where you can see our methodology in full. But for now, I just want to give you an impression of scale.

To date, we've created, collected, and analyzed the data from almost 750,000 online surveys (and counting) conducted around the world, using a team of translators fluent in 152 languages. That's a lot of surveys. And they've all been read by a human, without help from any AI or machine learning or metaverse robots from another dimension.

What's even more mind-boggling is that the surveys were customized based on how each respondent answered each question. If you answered the first question a certain way, it would lead you to a different second question than if you had answered otherwise, and so on, with the response to each question triggering the next set of questions you would see.

We conducted the survey in two stages—Canada and the United States first, and then the rest of the world—and we course-corrected as we went along. Our aim was simple: to create the first global map of core human values.

For ultimate statistical geekiness, you can tell people the Valuegraphics Database is +/- 3.5% accurate with a 95% level of confidence. But it's far easier to say that it's more accurate than you'd need to earn a PhD from any Ivy League university on the planet. In other words, it's bulletproof. It had to be because we are seriously rocking the demographic boat.

In our quest to create the Valuegraphics Database, we discovered the outrageous inaccuracies of demographic profiling. Turns out, people who share a demographic label are incredibly different from each other and don't share the same values at all. That finding tends to upset a lot of people—consultants who make a living by being the millennial whisperer or writing books about how Generation Z are rare unicorns in the enchanted forest that we have never seen before. These experts come running at me with guns a-blazing all the time and understandably so. We now have undeniable proof that generational stereotypes are nonsense—proof that puts them out of work. In fact, broad-sweeping stereotypes based on any demographic label are jaw-droppingly inaccurate.

Here is a look at the data.

THE DEATH OF DEMOGRAPHIC STEREOTYPES

There are two macro facts that we should get out of the way before we start looking at more granular numbers. These are two data-driven conclusions we've drawn from the database that you might want to commit to memory for whenever someone tries to defend demographic profiling. Think of them as your first line of defense against the forces of wrong-headedness.

The first fact is this: around the world, people agree roughly 8% of the time. This means that no matter what values you use to engage an audience, you will find that roughly 8% of the population of planet Earth will be on board.

The second fact is this: people within any demographic cohort are aligned with each other, on average, 10.5% of the time. Put another way, any demographic group is, on average, only 10.5% cohesive. This is the fact that gets the disciples of demography all upset.

Millennials, baby boomers, men, women, rich, poor, married, single, divorced, widowed, one child or three—the people within each of these demographic buckets agree on the values that drive all their behaviors, decisions, and emotions roughly 10.5% of the time. That means they disagree 89.5% of the time.

Now let's combine those two facts. If demographic cohorts are 10.5% aligned, but we automatically have 8% alignment because that's how often all humans are marching to the beat of the same drum, then that means *demographic profiling is a mere 2.5% better than no profiling at all.*

Think about that. If you target married millennials who earn $100,000 and have two kids, you have a 2.5% better chance of attracting their attention, no matter what you do, than if you disregarded demographic profiling altogether and said whatever popped into your head.

Demographics are still important to describe what your target audience looks like. You still need demographics to put a metaphorical fence around a group of people that you are keen to engage.

But after we tabulated close to 750,000 highly accurate surveys from around the globe, we can now say that demographically similar people are as different from each other as snowflakes. Let's look at some of the demographic categories and labels we use to understand a target audience, and why they don't make any sense.

NOBODY ACTS THEIR AGE ANYMORE

According to Walt Disney, "Growing old is mandatory, but grow-ing up is optional." And the Valuegraphics Database backs him up.

As you scan the age cohort table below, remember that these numbers include an 8% alignment that's baked right in, because humans of all ages agree 8% of the time. For example, although millennials around the world agree with each other 14% of the time, they all agree with each other 8% of the time anyway. Targeting millennials nets out to be only 6% more powerful than targeting all age groups equally.

There are so many fascinating questions raised by these findings. The silent generation, for example—people born between 1928 and 1945—seem to be the most aligned of all the generations globally, except in Europe, where Gen Z wins the alignment sweepstakes, and Central/South America, where Gen Z and Gen X are tied for the top honors.

This point alone could be the subject of an entire additional study. Why, in Europe, are members of Gen Z more similar than all other age groups? And why Gen Z *and* Gen X in Central/South America? You might argue that the youngest among us are more similar because of the flattening forces of technology. But then, why wouldn't that be the case in other parts of the world? It would be illuminating to dive deeper and learn more because something else seems to be lurking in the data here, waiting to be found out.

Here are a few interesting points raised by this data:

- The oldest and youngest generations around the world are the most aligned.

- Regardless of age, the people in the Middle East resemble each other the most.

- Across all generations, the people of Africa are the least alike.

You can point to these numerical patterns in the age data and ask questions about what they might mean all day long. But the big takeaway is that people within any age cohort are shockingly, reassuringly unalike. It's shocking because even though we all sort of knew that nobody acts their age anymore, I don't think we realized to what extent. And it's reassuring because I for one am glad for statistical proof that using age to define who people are is officially bunk. Because ageism is a problem of epic proportions.

There is a growing chorus of voices calling for an end to ageist practices in contemporary life, but ageism as a discriminatory practice has yet to be fully exposed and addressed. Most of the energy in the anti-ageism movement is currently centered on disrupting discriminatory recruitment and hiring practices that sideline older job applicants. And I wholeheartedly applaud those efforts. But little attention is devoted to eradicating the problem across all age categories.

Being mean to our elders is like hurting a puppy: it's easy to drum up outrage. But we must remember that this can't be only about our elders; otherwise, the anti-ageism movement would itself be based on ageist ideas. Look at the youngest age cohorts (which, for our purposes, begin at age 18). Younger people, regardless of their individual merit, routinely face discrimination solely based on their age.

- Younger people pay more for car insurance because risk assessment models demographically classify people, and obviously all young people are equally, uniformly terrible drivers.

- Landlords favor more mature tenants because of an assumption that they will be quieter. They've clearly never met some of my boisterous, well-past-age-50 friends and neighbors.

- And even though this one will get me in trouble with some people, why is it OK for labor unions to guarantee job protection and promotions on seniority rather than skill?

In all aspects of life, and for all ages, we need to continually paraphrase Tina Turner and ask ourselves, "What's age got to do with it?"

VALUES ALIGNMENT/COHESION BY AGE					
Region	Gen Z (1996–2012*)	Millennials (1980–1995)	Gen X (1965–1979)	Boomers (1946–1964)	Silents (1925–1945)
World	16%	14%	15%	13%	18%
USA	16%	15%	12%	14%	17%
North America (ex USA)	16%	15%	11%	13%	17%
Europe	18%	13%	12%	14%	13%
China	18%	13%	14%	15%	19%
Asia (ex China)	13%	11%	15%	15%	18%
Oceania	11%	13%	18%	14%	21%
Middle East	17%	19%	20%	17%	18%
Africa	10%	11%	12%	14%	17%
Central/South America	17%	14%	17%	11%	13%

THE BATTLE OF THE SEXES

According to the *Farlex Dictionary of Idioms*, the Battle of the Sexes is a phrase that refers to "the ongoing struggles and conflicts that exist between men and women."[2]

We've all heard this phrase before; it permeates our culture. In reality, however, neither men nor women are similar enough to each other to be united on any issue, never mind teaming up to battle each other. In fact, when it comes to what people care about and what they value, men and women are statistically identical.

It would be inconceivable to talk about the Battle of the Shoe Sizes, which might be defined as "the ongoing struggle between people who wear at least a size 10 shoe versus those with smaller feet." It's laughable because, as we'd say to ourselves, *It's ridiculous to think that people with big feet are all united around different things than smaller-footed folks.* And we'd be 100% right for thinking that. You can't group people together based on physical characteristics and assume they will be similar to each other. And yet we do. We do it over and over again with gender.

So a big round of applause to the editors of the Free Dictionary for concluding that *"men and women have some general differences, but the battle of the sexes is really just perpetuated by our outdated ideas of gender."*[3]

Let's look at what the numbers say.

The table below shows how similar men are to each

---

2 *Farlex Dictionary of Idioms*, "Battle of the sexes," quoted in The Free Dictionary, "the battle of the sexes," https://idioms.thefreedictionary.com/Battle+of+the+sexes

3 *Farlex Dictionary of Idioms*, "Battle of the sexes," quoted in The Free Dictionary, "the battle of the sexes," https://idioms.thefreedictionary.com/Battle+of+the+sexes

other and how similar women are to each other. The numbers are equally low for both genders. Once you deduct the 8% alignment that all humans share, regardless of gender, the results are even less significant.

It follows, then, that the Battle of the Sexes is a nonsensical idea, as you can't have a battle between two groups that aren't groups. It also makes any targeting decision you might make based on gender highly suspect.

Most curious of all to me are the target audience descriptions that include a blended total—something like "60% male and 40% female." Maybe the CRM system for your brand of sleeping pills, wax paper, or artichoke hearts can track gender, and perhaps past purchases have originated from an audience with a 60/40 gender split. But who cares? The more useful question is why? Why did some men and some women buy your product? Figure that out and you can move forward with traction, instead of seductively familiar but wholly inaccurate gender stereotypes.

Looking at the results region by region, we see a few aberrant statistics. In the Middle East, for example, the similarity among men is 4% greater than it is around the world. In China, men resemble each other 3% more often. But when the most extreme examples we can point to are so low to begin with, you have to ask yourself, "When it comes to understanding your customers, why bother talking about gender cohorts at all?"

Curiously, women in China are more alike by 8% than women around the rest of the world. But honestly, who cares? It's academically interesting but practically useless.

As I've pointed out repeatedly, demographic labels like gender are still useful, and in some cases necessary, to define a target audience. To be silly and make a point, some intimate personal care products found at the pharmacy are meant only for men or only for women because of biological realities. However, using gender as a way to understand what makes a particular target audience buy one brand versus another? That's beyond silly. It's wrong.

VALUES ALIGNMENT/COHESION BY GENDER		
Region	Male	Female
World	14%	11%
USA	13%	12%
North America (ex USA)	13%	11%
Europe	11%	9%
China	17%	19%
Asia (ex China)	10%	11%
Oceania	13%	14%
Middle East	18%	11%
Africa	13%	14%
Central/South America	12%	12%

THE RICH ARE DIFFERENT FROM YOU AND ME

F. Scott Fitzgerald started one of his most famous stories, "The Rich Boy," by pointing out that the rich are different—a thought that captured a stereotype from the public consciousness and preserved it like a fly in amber. The actual sentence Fitzgerald wrote was, "Let me tell you about the very rich. They are different from you and me."[4]

But if Fitzgerald wanted to make a completely accurate observation of the human condition, he would need to point out that the very rich are also different from each other.

According to *Forbes* magazine, Bernard Arnault has accumulated roughly $150 billion as chairman and CEO of LVMH, the company that owns 70 luxury brands, including Louis Vuitton and Sephora.[5] How values-aligned do you suppose he is to fellow multibillionaire Qin Yinglin, who, at number 14 on the *Forbes* list of billionaires, is the world's wealthiest pig farmer?[6]

To be fair, maybe they share a lot in common, and maybe they don't—and that's kind of the point. You can't tell anything about who these two men are by knowing they both have billions and billions of dollars. You can only know how they look at the world if you know what they care about or what they value—because those values are the root cause of everything they do.

Around the world and in each region individually, people agree with each other slightly more if they earn more. But as with all the demographic categories we have examined in our global study, the most extreme examples are not all that extreme.

Let's look at those who earn more than $250,000 a year, specifically in the Middle East. Why this group? Because

4   F. Scott Fitzgerald, "The Rich Boy," *Red Book* (Jan.–Feb. 1926), https://gutenberg.net.au/fsf/the-rich-boy.html

5   Forbes Profile, "Bernard Arnault & Family," 2022, https://www.forbes.com/profile/bernard-arnault/?sh=37846af266fa

6   Forbes Profile, "Qin Yinglin," 2002, https://www.forbes.com/profile/qin-yinglin/?sh=24b4cafa6365

this is the most aligned group we found. In fact, *across all demographic labels, this is the most aligned cohort of all.* They agree with each other 22% of the time.

Let's subtract 8% because that's how much all humans agree with each other. That leaves us with a score of 14%. People in the most-aligned, most-cohesive cohort on the entire planet agree with each 14% more than they agree with anyone else on earth.

That's the biggest gun in the arsenal of anyone who still believes demographics are an accurate way to categorize people and understand who they are. It's hardly a gun at all. It's a broken plastic toy water pistol, maybe. But nothing more.

VALUES ALIGNMENT/COHESION BY INCOME				
Region	<$50k	$50k to $100k	$100k to $250k	$250k+
World	12%	13%	13%	17%
USA	5%	8%	11%	17%
North America (ex USA)	4%	9%	13%	19%
Europe	7%	10%	14%	17%
China	11%	14%	14%	21%
Asia (ex China)	8%	9%	11%	12%
Oceania	10%	9%	8%	16%
Middle East	14%	14%	15%	22%
Africa	17%	21%	14%	17%
Central/South America	19%	14%	11%	7%

GOING TO THE CHAPEL

Relationship status—whether we are married, single, divorced, or widowed—is another favorite set of demographic labels used in boardrooms everywhere to help understand a target audience.

I know you can't see me, so I'll tell you that right now, my eyes are rolling back into my head. It's preposterous to think that somehow, miraculously, everyone who is married resembles each other.

Sure, married people (in Westernized cultures, at least) have all had a big ceremony and an awkward party where relatives and college roommates all drank too much. But otherwise, how could anyone think all married couples are alike?

Of course married couples will likely be shopping for certain things, like the mandatory decorative throw cushions for the matrimonial sofa, but *why* they choose one brand of cushion over another will be based on their values.

Now think about all the single people you know. Any resemblance there, other than their singleness? Highly unlikely.

And of course, the Valuegraphics Database backs up what common sense confirms. No matter how you slice the data, being hitched or not hitched does not sort people into groups that resemble each other in any meaningful way.

I am, however, curious about a couple of things that the data revealed. Have a look at the global statistics for similarity within a cohort, which is the first line in the chart below. Notice that people who are widowed are the least similar to each other of all. But they were once married, and married people are among the *most* similar global cohorts. So what happened?

Why is it that those who lost a spouse are suddenly veering off and becoming less alike than they were before? The margin of difference is so small that it's barely a blip on the radar of important findings, but even so, it's an interesting conversation starter for your next dinner party.

And if we want even more dinner-party trivia, here's something fun. In North America, married people have similar values 7% of the time. Which means if you subtract the 8% that all humans resemble each other regardless of their demographic profile, married people in North America share a small deficit of similarity. Opposites really do attract.

VALUES ALIGNMENT/COHESION BY RELATIONSHIP STATUS					
Region	Married/Living in Relationship	Committed, Living Apart	Happily Single	Grumpy Single	Widowed
World	12%	9%	11%	12%	6%
USA	9%	10%	13%	8%	5%
North America (ex USA)	7%	8%	14%	9%	6%
Europe	11%	14%	18%	6%	7%
China	14%	9%	11%	19%	8%
Asia (ex China)	15%	11%	11%	15%	11%
Oceania	9%	14%	10%	15%	7%
Middle East	16%	7%	9%	7%	6%
Africa	11%	9%	12%	11%	11%
Central/South America	10%	13%	14%	13%	12%

PARENTAL ADVISORY

I'm writing this during Betwixtmas, that strange period of timeless time between Christmas and New Year's Eve. Consequently, I have been spending a lot of time on social media, scrolling around voyeuristically and watching what my friends and acquaintances are doing.

A good number of my social media friends have kids. Although it's not a statistically accurate sample to draw conclusions from, if I analyze the narratives they construct about the state of parenthood, I see two distinct camps.

First are the parents who want me to believe that having kids is a jolly big bunch of fun and that their kids are cuddly, hilarious kooks. Pet owners take this stance frequently on social media, too.

The second group presents the responsibilities of parenthood as a kind of Sisyphean task, a never-ending struggle to persevere against enormous odds. They talk about their exhaustion, make frequent references to wine and weed as essential weapons to help them get through it all, and grossly overuse the palms-up-shoulder-shrug emoji to show how they have no control over the trajectory of their days.

These polar-opposite characterizations—entertained versus beleaguered—are best thought of as bookends on a long bookshelf with a million books between them that represent all the various realities of what it means to be a parent. In fact, there are likely as many versions of what parenthood is about as there are parents. Using nothing but logic, it's safe to say that no two sets of parents are the same.

And guess what. Once again, the data backs up what we all know to be true. The presence of kids in your life is not a reliable indicator of how similar you are to others in the same situation.

But despite the low levels of alignment within a cohort, the variances from one cohort to the next offer up all kinds of speculative fun. For example, single parents with one kid in the EU are more than twice as similar to each other than their counterparts in Central/South America, Africa, or Oceania. What do you suppose is behind that? Parenthood in the EU seems to attract a smaller but more aligned slice of the population. In other regions of the world, perhaps what it means to be a parent is open to more broad interpretation and therefore attracts people with a broader base of values.

VALUES ALIGNMENT/COHESION BY NUMBER OF CHILDREN					
Region	One Child, Single Parent	Two or More Children, Single Parent	One Child, Two Parents	Two or More Children, Two Parents	No Children
World	12%	11%	7%	9%	6%
USA	16%	12%	5%	8%	6%
North America (ex USA)	17%	13%	7%	9%	4%
Europe	19%	11%	7%	10%	7%
China	15%	13%	9%	7%	11%
Asia (ex China)	11%	14%	17%	12%	9%
Oceania	9%	9%	11%	13%	14%
Middle East	13%	11%	8%	6%	6%
Africa	8%	14%	11%	9%	5%
Central/South America	8%	14%	7%	12%	7%

EDUCATION IS THE PASSPORT TO THE FUTURE

"Education is the passport to the future, for tomorrow belongs to those who prepare for it today,"[7] as Malcolm X famously said, but having the travel documents required

---

7 Malcolm X, "Speech at Founding Rally of the Organization of Afro-American Unity (June 28, 1964)," as quoted in By Any Means Necessary (1970), https://quotepark.com/quotes/1169564-malcolm-x-education-is-our-passport-to-the-future-for-tomor/

for a better tomorrow does not mean you resemble others who have those credentials, too.

What do Miuccia Prada; Martin Luther King Jr; and Carey, the guy from the gardening store at the end of my block have in common? They all have PhDs, which is quite likely where the similarities end. Educational achievements are not an accurate way to profile who people are, how they view the world, or why they decide to do the things they do.

Yet the table below does show similarities—how come? For exactly the same reason we had a room full of people buying those condos: they share values. The people we went to school with had to share at least some of our values, and those values are represented in the table below.

VALUES ALIGNMENT/COHESION BY LEVEL OF EDUCATION

Region	None	Some Formal, but Didn't Finish	Bachelors or Equivalent	Postgrad +
World	13%	14%	16%	9%
USA	12%	12%	12%	4%
North America (ex USA)	11%	12%	13%	7%
Europe	9%	9%	16%	10%
China	16%	17%	13%	8%
Asia (ex China)	15%	14%	17%	14%
Oceania	11%	9%	15%	6%
Middle East	10%	11%	13%	15%
Africa	14%	8%	9%	11%
Central/South America	14%	8%	11%	8%

Here's something to stare at the ceiling and think about. Around the world, we agree with each other more as our education level increases. This is logical, because some marginal increase in values alignment drove each cohort to behave in the way they did and move on to the next step on the education ladder.

But then it all falls apart at the postgraduate level. People with a postgraduate degree are the least similar of all.

CAN WE AGREE THAT DEMOGRAPHICS ARE DONE?

I hope I've shown you across this chapter and the last how demographics don't really show us anything meaningful about who people are. We hold on to demographic thinking because it's how we're historically programmed to understand the world, and we've been so far unwilling to see it as a flawed model.

But it is a flawed model. The data proves it. Psychographics face the same limitation—they are historic records that do not help us understand how to influence what people do next. And when it comes to marketing, all that matters is how to influence what people do next.

What does offer us a measure of certainty around influencing the future is shared values. Each one of the not-Bob & Sally condo buyers in my opening story purchased a condo because our marketing accidentally aligned with their values. And as I'll further reveal in the next section, values are the only driver of human behavior.

PART TWO

FUNDAMENTALS
OF
VALUEGRAPHICS

CHAPTER 3

THE THREE-LEGGED STOOL OF AUDIENCE INSIGHTS

INSTEAD OF THE USUAL DEMOGRAPHIC-CENTRIC PROFILES of target audiences, think about a three-legged stool of audience insights.

Demographics are a great place to start. The $20 million penthouse condominium at the top of the new luxury tower in downtown Gotham City will not sell to an 18-year-old grocery store clerk. It's a pretty safe bet that the penthouse buyers will be a married couple of a certain age who have a certain amount of money. That's a demographic reality that's important to know. It doesn't tell you everything you need to know, but think of it as one leg of a three-legged stool.

The second leg of our three-legged stool is psychographics. Psychographics may tell us that our penthouse condominium buyers have multiple homes, enjoy entertaining, and are patrons of the arts. All interesting stuff, but it still leaves us guessing how to make your penthouse irresistible.

To truly understand how to engage and activate a target audience, you need the third leg of the three-legged stool. You need to understand which core human values are driving the buyer's decisions, behaviors, and emotions. You need their valuegraphics.

Some of those penthouse buyers will care deeply for *Family* and would love to see a climbing wall, a small swimming pool on the roof deck, and a media room with surround sound because, in the eyes of their grandkids, this would make them the coolest grandparents ever.

Others won't place a high value on *Family* but will want the materials used in their suite to be carbon neutral. They'd be drawn to the xenon gas insulated triple-pane windows because of the value they place on *Environmentalism*.

And some might be looking for a home that boosts their *Social Standing* or fuels the value they place on *Ambition*, in which case ostrich leather walls, exotic tigerwood floors, and an industrial-grade catering kitchen might be the right direction to go.

Demographics describe the outward-facing characteristics of a target audience, and psychographics record relevant insights from the past. But for a sturdy three-legged stool to stand on, you also need valuegraphics.

Let's look at this through the lens of marketing a hypothetical chocolate bar. Imagine a room filled with 100 people. Let's say they are all men, and they are between the ages of 37 and 45. They are married with two kids. They have white-collar jobs in the financial services industry and earn $100,000 a year. Let's say they all have a university degree. You can add on as many other demographic layers to this description as you like.

It's your job to sell these men a chocolate bar. It can be a chocolate bar of any kind because you get to invent it from scratch. And you can say anything you want to them about the chocolate bar as long as it convinces them to buy one.

You might start by asking yourself, *Do they even like chocolate bars? What kinds do they buy, and how often?* So you commission a study. The results come back: they like Kit Kat bars best of all, and they buy one every week.

It's time to decide what to do. You have a target audience description that includes demographic information, and the psychographic insights that your study revealed. What kind of chocolate bar will appeal to 37- to 45-year-old white-collar, married men who earn $100,000 a year, have two kids, and eat a Kit Kat once a week? Further, what could you say to them about that chocolate bar to get them to buy it?

Sports! you think to yourself. *Middle-aged family guys like sports!* So you negotiate with the NBA for permission to use their logo and make a chocolate bar called HOOPS.

Equally plausible, you might decide that these men are at an age where they don't have the energy they used to have. So you make a chocolate bar loaded with caffeine and call it SLAM DUNK. You like this idea because it has sports *plus* the promise of more energy!

You might test these ideas with a few focus groups. Overwhelmingly, everyone likes SLAM DUNK best, and you think you have a winning idea on your hands.

Based on demographics and a few psychographic insights, you launch your chocolate bar and cross your fingers that you have done the right thing. You need to keep those fingers crossed because what you have done supposes that your audience likes sports and wants energy in the form of a chocolate snack.

It seems like a safe bet. And it scores well when tested. But of all the chocolate bars you could have created, is that the most universally appealing? Or is it simply the best of the two possible options you put forward to focus groups for an opinion?

This is how marketing has traditionally been done. We look at the demographics, add a few psychographic insights, and assume we have enough knowledge from the data to tell us what our target audience might care about so that we can accurately predict whether they'll buy our product or not. But as we showed in Part One, demographics don't really tell us anything about who people are and what they'll do next. Maybe you'll sell a lot of chocolate bars, and maybe you won't. But if you do, it'll be a happy accident—a bunch of guesswork.

Now let's say you add one extra audience insight to the target audience profile before you settle on what kind of bar to make and how to go to market. Let's say you knew just one core human value that your target audience shared in common: *Health & Well-Being*.

Suddenly, the path to convincing your target audience to buy your chocolate bar is much easier to follow and relies on far less intuition and guesswork. If your chocolate bar helps those white-collar married guys achieve more *Health & Well-Being* and the marketing strategy reinforces that position, you have reduced the risk associated with your new product launch considerably.

Here's an idea. According to the American Cancer Society,[8] chocolate may help prevent heart disease. Flavanols in chocolate have been shown to lower blood pressure and make your heart, veins, and arteries work better.

Your chocolate bar could be formulated to contain twice the normal amount of flavanols. You decide to call it the HEART BAR. And inside the wrapper, like fortunes in a fortune cookie, are a series of facts from various academic studies about how the ingredients in this chocolate bar will help you live a healthier and longer life. That way, while you enjoy your chocolate, you can reassure yourself that you've made a brilliant choice and that this treat is very good for you. Scientists agree, after all, and who are you to argue with science?

Your risk is substantially reduced as soon as you know *even one shared value* of the target group. Now you could laser-focus on developing a product and a marketing approach that gives your 100 men more of what they already want—what they value most of all.

And consider this: the values-based idea would work regardless of demographics. There will be 19-year-old women in college who love the HEART BAR as much as

---

8   Stacy Simon, "Is Chocolate Good for You?" American Cancer Society, https://www.cancer.org/latest-news/is-chocolate-good-for-you.html

our fictitious target audience of white-collar men. Our research proves that values are demographically agnostic: *Health & Well-Being* will be highly valued by a cross section of chocolate lovers across all demographic cohorts.

CROSSING THE LAST MILE

Valuegraphics is key to bringing more certainty to the last mile.

Everyone knows data can only get you so far. There will always be a leap of intuition and educated guesswork needed to decide the final steps to take, or what we call the last mile. But demographics are descriptive and psychographics are *historic*. They describe people and tell you what they've done so far. But they don't tell you *why* they do things and how they'll decide what to do next.

Valuegraphics tell you the root of people's decisions and the drivers of their behavior. If you use the three-legged stool of audience insights, there will still be a gap between the data and how you use it—a gap that experience, intuition, and street smarts must fill. But that gap is much smaller. It's no longer a last mile; we've brought it down to the last 100 yards because what we value determines everything we do.

In the next chapter, we'll explore how values act as drivers of our decisions, and we'll take a crash course in the science that backs it up.

CHAPTER 4

WHAT WE VALUE DETERMINES EVERYTHING WE DO

IT WAS A FRIDAY NIGHT IN THE MIDDLE OF WINTER. IT was one of those nights that a poet would call crystalline and crisp, but the rest of us would call damn cold. Three friends were heading home from the bar where they'd met after work. They weren't the type of friends who display their affection, but they hadn't seen each other in a few months and they had missed each other. They were glad to be together again. They had spent the last five hours sharing stories in an increasingly dramatic fashion that correlated directly to the amount of Japanese whiskey they consumed.

As the clock struck 12:00, they reluctantly agreed that it was time to call it a night and head home. They noisily made their way through the dark, laughing and goofing around, passing in and out of patches of light cast by overhead streetlamps, filled with flurries of snow.

Suddenly, they turned a corner and found themselves facing a dark alley. They fell silent for a moment. They had to decide what to do.

All we know about David is that his primary value—the thing he cares about more than anything else in life—is *Experiences*. He thinks it would be the absolute best idea in the world to go down that dark alley and see what happens. *This is perfect*, he thinks to himself. But he knows he will have to convince the others. He gives it his best shot. "Let's do this!" he yells excitedly, his eyes wide, his fist pumping the air. He is 100% ready to sprint down that alley and into the unknown.

All we know about Greg is that his primary value is *Security*. The sight of that dark alley instantly makes the hair on the back of his neck stand up. He is alert for danger, suddenly more sober than he was a moment ago. *This alley is trouble*, he thinks to himself. *These two knuckleheads are in no shape to walk down a hallway, let alone a dark alley at midnight in the middle of a blizzard.* "Let's go back," he declares in his most convincing voice. "Let's go back to the bar and have one more drink. We need one more."

And finally, there's Corey. All we know about Corey is

that he values *Friendship* more than anything else. "You guys decide," he says. "I don't care one way or the other." And he doesn't. He is equally willing to head down the alley into the great unknown or go back to the cozy confines of the bar. "I don't care as long as we stick together," he mutters to himself as he pulls the other two into a hug. "We stay together, OK? I love you guys."

Three friends must make a decision, and three reasonable conclusions are reached. Each friend behaves in a way that aligns with his values, because what we value determines everything we do.

Moreover, demographics had nothing to do with it. Not one of those boozy buddies had to check in and see if they were young or old, rich or poor, had a college degree, or a family before deciding what to do.

All we need to know in order to understand how these buddies will behave is what they value.

Let's say it was your job as the vice president of marketing at Dark Alley Enterprises to convince a target audience of people to go down that dark alley.

If you knew your target audience placed a high value on *Experiences*, you'd know exactly how to entice them to pay the price of admission and enjoy the dark alley. You'd convince them it was the most exciting dark alley on earth and that a team of Dark Alley Enterprises Imagineers had spent years planning and building this alley. It was jam-packed with all the signature thrills and unexpected chills that only a genuine Dark Alley Experience™ could offer.

If you knew your target audience highly valued *Security*, you'd have a different pitch prepared. You could start by pointing out the inevitability of encountering dark alleys as we live our best lives, which is why you developed the unique Dark Alley Safety Net™ protocols: to remove all the risks associated with dark alley use. Pressure-sensitive emergency lighting would turn on and off automatically as you walked through the dark alley. And Ollie, a voice-activated digital assistant, would always be there to help you, easily summoned with the audio command, "Hey, Ollie."

And finally, if you knew your target audience was united around the value of *Friendship*? In that case, the dark alley would be an amazing opportunity to help those three friends break free of Western civilization's rigid codes of masculine behavior and build closer bonds. In the Dark Alley Friendship Challenge™ various tests must be completed to allow the trio to move further along the alley to the next level, like a three-dimensional role-playing game. Trust falls, blindfolded food tasting, interpretive dance therapy, ropes courses, Lego-based emotional visualizations...the possibilities are endless. For all the Coreys who value *Friendship* so highly, the brand promise would be clear and irrefutable: this alley will bring you closer to each other.

In fact, if those *Friendship* challenges could be wrapped up in a blanket of *Safety* and presented as a series of exciting *Experiences*, you'd have a triple-threat proposition that all three target audiences—the Davids and Gregs and Coreys—would find irresistibly magnetic. They would go down that dark alley, guaranteed.

This certainty about the central importance of values is not a fluffy philosophical idea. It's grounded in decades of rigorous research and across multiple fields of scientific inquiry.

THE UNIFYING CONCLUSION OF BEHAVIORAL SCIENCE

Behavioral science is a broad term that attempts to link together several individual fields of scientific inquiry: psychology, sociology, and neurology, to name a few. These disciplines each have their own focus, and practitioners often disagree on the most fundamental things. But they are all, in one way or another, concerned with understanding how humans behave and how they interact with one another.

If you start googling the subject matter discussed in these next paragraphs, you will end up immersed in a world of scientific studies and published articles that stretch back over decades. I'll leave that for the most intrepid readers to explore on their own. For the purposes of this book, I want to focus on one unifying connection between the work of countless scientists over decades of time: the incredible power of human values as a determinant of behavior. Put another way: what we value determines what we do.

Values and Neuroscience

You will often hear people talking about the prefrontal cortex of the human brain as the "CEO" of the brain. It's an apt comparison because the CEO of any organization is responsible for considering available information and then making decisions about what to do next. And that's what your prefrontal cortex does. It sorts and sifts through all the incoming information you are bombarded with in the course of a day and then issues directives about what to do next. All your behaviors, emotions, and decisions begin with the work of the prefrontal cortex.[9]

Neuroscientists will tell you that your prefrontal cortex uses one overriding set of filters to determine how to respond to incoming data. That set of filters? The things we care about most, otherwise known as our values.

If you decide to buy a car, it will be because of a set of values your prefrontal cortex is using to evaluate the various options. One car might signal *Social Standing*, another *Environmentalism,* and a third might feel aligned with the importance you place on *Health & Well-Being.* Your choice will be driven by the values that are most important to you.

Should you go to bed early and be fresh for the exam you have in the morning, or should you stay up late to have drinks with your friends? Your decision will be based on some interplay of the values that are most important to you, the things you care about most.

Humans are neurologically hardwired to chase after the things they care about, the things they value. In other words, neuroscientists agree that what we value determines what we do.

Values and Psychology

Psychological tests like the MMPI Inventory and the Myers-Briggs test (and many others) help psychologists identify your core values. Then psychologists work with you to ensure your life and your values are aligned because that's what makes a happy and well-adjusted person.

---

9 Alarik Arenander, "CEO of the Brain: Brain Coherence: The Ultimate Competitive Edge," n.d., accessed August 29, 2022, https://theleadersbrain.org/overview/ceo.html

In fact, the values-centric existence that humans share is so powerful that psychologists engaged in research must find workarounds that help them avoid it. Surveys must be designed to avoid *confirmation bias*, which is the natural human tendency to agree with anything that confirms what we already value. If you aren't careful, confirmation bias can mess up survey results by preventing impartial answers.

Psychologists are on the same page as neurologists when it comes to values. Humans are magnetically drawn toward the things they value because what we value determines what we do.

Values and Sociology

Sociologists study the behavior of large groups of people. The Valuegraphics Database is a sociological dataset.

Why did so many people vote for a seemingly peculiar candidate in an election? Why does an entire subculture of people flock to Burning Man every year? Why do vegans exist? As I am sure you have guessed, the answer to these sociological questions always comes down to values.

Voters decided that their peculiar candidate was the man for the job because he promised a future where "people like us" who "share our values" would prosper. Once a candidate has successfully activated the shared values of a segment of the population, he or she can do or say nearly anything and his or her fan club will follow along. Values are that powerful. Once harnessed, they can carry an underdog to victory.

Why do people go to Burning Man, an anti-establishment

weeklong party in the middle of the desert, famous for psychedelically enhanced romps and enormous ad hoc art installations primarily made of sticks?

It's not because of how old they are or their gender, income, education, or marital status. In fact, the people at Burning Man each year come from all walks of life. Some arrive on foot, and others land their private jets at the nearest airport. Demographics will not help you understand why these celebrants are here.

Furthermore, psychographic analysis of the crowd at Burning Man might tell you how many are repeat visitors, which experience-enhancing substances are preferred, or what kind of music will keep them dancing longest. All of this is fascinating, but still, none of it explains why they attend. What drives these people? What's the connective tissue? What's the throughline that makes this group of people a group?

What they share in common, of course, is a set of values that Burning Man delivers on. That's why they are there. Perhaps—and I'm guessing here—values like *Belonging, Creativity, Health & Well-Being, Friendship*, and even *Personal Growth* are strong for this target audience. That's a powerful combination of irresistibly magnetic reasons to attend.

And how about vegans? What makes people decide to eat nothing but plants? Demographics and psychographics won't help you here. Vegans pop up all over the place when you least expect it. And there will be various subsegments to consider, too. I have not studied vegans to be able to say this with any authority, but let's pretend we had studied them and that *Social Standing* had risen to the top of the values profile. Wouldn't that be a shocker? Not *Environmentalism*, as one would expect, or even *Health & Well-Being*, which would be a sensible guess, but *Social Standing*. What if the vegans who were attracted to your product, service, or brand were doing it for show? What if it was nothing more than virtue signaling? Wouldn't that be an incredibly powerful thing to know?

I've flown off on a bit of a tangent here, so let me bring this narrative home to roost. Sociologists are holding hands with neurologists and psychologists on this point: they all agree that the only way to understand why people do things is by identifying their values because what we value determines what we do.

CHAPTER 5

THE VALUEGRAPHICS DATABASE

EVERY ORGANIZATION ON EARTH WANTS TO CONVINCE some people to do something. And people will only do things that give them more of what they value. So, to be successful, an organization must identify what people value and give them as much of that as they can. You can see how powerful values are when it comes to marketing, product creation, and closing that last mile.

Behavioral scientists have known about the magnetic power of values for a long time, but what was missing was a Rosetta stone that would crack the code and make this knowledge operational for organizations to use. That's what the Valuegraphics Database was made to do. It's the first database that maps the values that drive all human behavior, everywhere on earth, and can pinpoint which values any group of people share in common.

You'll recall we mentioned this database in Chapter 2, when we talked about how our research showed the fallacy of demographic profiles. Creating this database was an enormous undertaking and quite the adventure, partly because we first had to *identify* which values were driving the behaviors of everyone on earth. This is what makes this database such a breakthrough. It's the first complete inventory of shared human values, a kind of directory of how humans make decisions. Put another way, it's the operating system for being human.

Here's how we put the database together.

BUILDING THE VALUEGRAPHICS DATABASE

The Valuegraphics Database is the result of more than three-quarters of a million online surveys (and counting) conducted around the world, using a team of translators fluent in 152 languages. Even more interesting, the surveys were designed to react and change based on how the respondent answered. You could think of these surveys as three-dimensional, with each answer potentially triggering the next question to come at you by drilling down, moving along the same level, or shifting to an entirely new line of questions. This unlimited variation in question-pathing is one of the most exciting things about the brave new world of online/digital surveys. Simpler, old-fashioned surveys only allow questions to follow one after the other in a sequence, or perhaps skip ahead a bit using the familiar phrase, "If you answered no to this question, skip ahead to question 5." Yawn.

Furthermore, there were 10 different sets of survey questions that focused on 10 different themes. For example, one theme was sports, fitness, health, and recreation. In all, we had 10 different surveys each, with multiple three-dimensional variations based on the way each respondent answered each question. Still with me?

The Questions We Asked

Using the 10 themes as a starting point, we asked respondents all over the world about their wants, needs, and expectations from life. Because of the three-dimensional nature of the survey design, the responses we received to this series of questions became a contextualizing layer of 380 possible data points. These 380 metrics about wants, needs, and expectations helped us better understand how the backbone of the study—the core human values that are most important to people—could be fleshed out.

For example, it's one thing to know that *Family* is the most important value in someone's life. But it helps us understand how *Family* is impacting behaviors and emotions if we also know their wants, needs, and expectations when it comes to their family.

As for the values themselves, in order to map their importance for the population of planet Earth, we had to have a list of values to start with. We looked to respected social science studies like the World Values Index and the Bhutan Gross Domestic Happiness Index and came up with a list of 40 values to track.

For practical reasons, we began by mapping these values for the United States and Canada. That's what my last book, *We Are All the Same Age Now*, was about. We started using this preliminary dataset for two countries to profile target audiences for clients and to generate reports on various industries. At the same time, we quietly finished our work polling the populations of the other countries of the world.

At the time, it felt frustrating that we couldn't do the entire planet all at once. This two-step approach was necessary to pay the bills and fund the completion of the global dataset. But in retrospect, I'm glad it happened this way because we learned so much from using the database on a smaller scale before we went global.

Crunching through all the global survey responses made it abundantly clear that the initial list of values we had been using for Canada and the United States needed an upgrade. There were more values at play around the world than we, or anyone else, had ever suspected. This is worth waving a flag about. It's not every day that a new value is identified, after all.

Many things that we had assumed were behaviors, beliefs, or mere interests turned out to be core values. A behavior, belief, or interest becomes important enough to be labeled a core value when it influences all the emotions and behaviors of a significant segment of a population. When something rules the lives of enough people, it has become a value.

For example, *Environmentalism* was not a value on the master list when we started. It was merely something that some people were keen on. Thankfully for the future of the planet, there were enough people around the world for whom *Environmentalism* was a major influence in all aspects of their life, and it was elevated to a core human value.

We eventually found 16 new values to add to the original list of 40. This left us with a newly expanded total of 56 core human values that are at the center of the Valuegraphics Database.

Fifty-six. That's the magic number of values that drive everything we do.

It doesn't seem like a lot of values when you think of the feelings, emotions, decisions, and behaviors that those 56 values have conjured up and unleashed in the world. Those values have been responsible for starting wars and ending them. For starting romances and ending them. For first jobs, first dates, first promotions, and putting the first man on the moon.

Everything humans do is driven by our values. Our values make us who we are and determine what kind of world we create. So in an exceedingly macro way, valuegraphics have created the physical world we see around us every day.

If we add up the 56 core human values and those 380 wants, needs, and expectations, we get a total of 436 metrics.

How We Asked those Questions

Research geeks like to call what we did a qual-quant survey. Qual-quant is a shorter and easier-to-say version of qualitative-quantitative, and it simply means that whereas some of the questions were multiple choice or based on rankings or other numeric inputs, other questions required text-based responses.

I'm snacking on cheese as I write this, so let's run with that as an example. Instead of listing five kinds of cheese, asking people to rank them, and moving along to the next topic, we'd go deeper. We'd ask people to tell us how they feel about their favorite cheese. What would it be like if they could have more of that cheese? What if they suddenly had less? And so on. In other words, people were prompted to offer insights about the cheese they love most of all.

Once we had all the text-based survey responses in front of us, we'd start looking for related ideas. And as much as we like to think every person on earth is unique, there are only so many possible ways to respond to a question about cheese, so eventually a pattern of responses would emerge. And, of course, once you can see a pattern, you can use numbers to capture it in the dataset and convert qualitative responses into quantitative data.

The Respondents

The data we collected is an accurate map of the values of nine regions of the world. Those nine regions include 180 countries out of a possible 185 at this moment in time. Countries are always inconveniently dissolving and forming, and so the total number in existence is not a static thing. Think of the map of the world that your elementary school teacher showed you in grade three and what that same map would look like today. Depending on how long ago you were in elementary school, those two maps will be significantly different.

The five countries we were not able to include in our dataset are countries like North Korea, where online survey distribution and collection is not a realistic undertaking for many reasons.

One thing that makes the Valuegraphics Database so unique is that the data was collected as a random stratified, statistically representative sample of those nine regions of the world. That's a bit of a tongue twister the first few times you try to say it out loud, and it's a real showstopper if you weave it into conversations at cocktail parties. It means that the data is a replica of the real world, with the same proportionate number of people of various age cohorts in each of the nine regions and those 180 countries but in miniature. I like to say it's our own little Lego model of the people of planet Earth.

People who know about statistics and representative samples will tell you how difficult it is to collect a random stratified, statistically representative sample of any population, even a small one. So when I tell these stats geeks that we have a random strat stat rep (that's how the cool kids say it) for the entire population of the world, they tend to light their hair on fire and run out of the room screaming. It's a big deal, and it's only been possible because of the algorithmic survey collection methods facilitated by social media.

Social media channels are, after all, the most sophisticated targeting tools ever created. They exist to allow advertisers to place an ad in front of a narrowly defined target group of people. Why not use the same geographic and demographic targeting capabilities for surveys? Once you get enough survey respondents of one kind, you can stop accepting any more of those and focus instead on recruiting more of the respondents that your sample is lacking.

At this point in the story, there's always someone who wants to tell me that sourcing survey respondents from social media leaves out everyone who is not on social media. That is why we sourced roughly 10% of the respondents using traditional survey respondent-sourcing methods. We did this to make sure the social media participants weren't somehow different from other people. We found that regardless of the source of the respondents, the responses were the same.

Oh, and let's not forget to talk about ethics. Survey respondents were not paid. They all knew why we were asking these questions, how we would use the data, and that we would anonymize their responses. To be extra-super-duper legit, we provided everyone with a secret code and an email address they could use to have their responses removed from the database at any time.

The Result

The result of this benchmark study is the Rosetta stone of valuegraphics. It's a database that accurately maps what people care about across the world. As we said in Chapter 2, the Valuegraphics Database is +/–3.5% accurate with a 95% level of confidence. In other words, it's empirically bulletproof.

The database establishes two very important things:

1. It proves that demographics are absolutely useless at describing *who* people are. Demographic stereotypes are bunk. If you need a refresher course, flip back to Chapter 2.

2. More importantly, it can identify the shared values of a target audience for anything in the world. This is important because shared values are the key to engaging a target audience, which is what all organizations are trying to do.

The Valuegraphics Profile

The Valuegraphics Database allows us to identify which of the 56 core human values a particular target audience shares. This list of shared values for a particular group is what we call a Valuegraphics Profile. You're going to see that term crop up a lot in the book from here on, so keep it in mind.

It's important to note that the groups profiled using valuegraphics can be anything. They could be baby boomers with a lot of money. They could be people who like to floss. They could be a region, like Africa. How we define a "group" will depend on what an organization is trying to do and who they want to engage and activate.

In the next chapter, we'll take a look at the 56 values that determine everything we do: the component parts of the Valuegraphics Database and building blocks of a Valuegraphics Profile.

CHAPTER 6

THE 56 VALUES THAT RUN YOUR LIFE

FIFTY-SIX VALUES DRIVE EVERYTHING HUMAN BEINGS DO.
These values define humanity. They are the operating system for being human. Understand them, and you understand what drives all our actions, everywhere on earth.

Over the last few years working with valuegraphic data, I've come to think of the 56 values as my friends.

Some are my best friends, and I see them turning up often—nearly every day, in fact. I know these friends intimately, and I can tell what's going on with them every time we are together. I can read them like a book.

Then there are some friends who I see only from

time to time. These friends are more like enjoyably close acquaintances.

And, of course, because nothing in this world is binary, I have a lot of friends who are somewhere in between those two extremes, whom I know with varying degrees of familiarity.

Moreover, like friends, the 56 values tend to cluster. Certain groups of values are always seen together, like the mean girls in high school, the steroidal bodybuilders at the gym, or the gossipy arts mavens. But values *can* surprise you—you never know which ones you might see together. Sometimes you'll be walking along, minding your own business, thinking about how comfortable your shoes are, when suddenly you see a bodybuilder having tea and croissants with an art maven at a table in a chic street café. The values universe is full of unexpected moments like that, which you can take as confusing or fascinating. I choose the latter.

Finally, there are the friends who have multiple personalities—not in the clinically diagnosed sense of the word, but you know who I mean. We all have that friend who veers between goofy jokes one day and lawyer-like seriousness the next.

DEFINING THE VALUES

Also, like friends, everyone will see these 56 values through a lens of personal experience. If you and I started talking about a mutual friend named Justin, we would both describe him differently. Our understanding would be based on our own personal experiences with him, what we'd heard other people saying, and what our gut said was likely to be true. Both your description and my description would be accurate but based on our different realities.

And that's exactly how the definitions for the 56 values work, too.

People quite naturally want to know how we define each of the 56 values. The answer is always the same: it's like talking about Justin. Everyone has a different idea of what each of the 56 values means, and they are all perfectly valid. We did not define the values at all. It's far more useful this way.

I don't care if you see yourself in a way that fits my definition of the value of *Creativity* or not. If I forced you to conform to my definition of *Creativity*, I'd be measuring how many people on earth see *Creativity* with the same lens as I do. Whereas what I want to know is who places a great deal of importance on whatever definition of *Creativity* they subscribe to and lives life accordingly.

Maybe you make macrame owl wall hangings with twigs for horns. Maybe your creative gift is seeing the patterns in financial statements and budgets. Or maybe you are a professional ballet dancer and a Star Trek memorabilia collector, and you see both of these pursuits as equally creative. What matters is that you believe you are creative and how the value you place on your own private version of *Creativity* influences everything you do.

When we profile an entire group of people this way, we see patterns in how they define the values that are most important to them. After that, all you need to do is connect the dots between your product, service, or brand and the *Creativity* they value.

In the chart that follows, I've inserted a comment where I have noticed something interesting or have an insight to offer. These broad-based notes are a kind of executive summary of how these values show up in the hundreds of profiles we've extrapolated from the Valuegraphics Database for various organizations in various sectors in various parts of the world.

THE 56 VALUES:
IN RANK ORDER OF IMPORTANCE FOR THE WORLD[10]

Rank	Value	Importance	Random Observations about This Value
1st	Family	84%	*Family* isn't only Mom, Dad, and the kids anymore. They come in all shapes and sizes, biological and otherwise.
2nd	Relationships	81%	*Relationships* are connections you have with people who range from your best friend to the barista you see every day who makes your triple Venti half-sweet nonfat caramel macchiato.
3rd	Financial Security	73%	Feeling secure financially means many different things to many different people. This will be an important value to some billionaires and to some minimum-wage workers.
4th	Belonging	70%	Feeling part of something: it could be a sports team you follow or a group of people you hang out with.
5th	Community	65%	Feeling a connection to something or some group, whether you are part of it or not.
6th	Personal Growth	62%	Wanting to be a better version of yourself.

10 The hypervigilant sociologist will point out that some of what we call values in this table are actually more accurately referred to as wants, needs, or expectations. I agree. However, for our purposes, we are referring to them as values because enough survey respondents around the world have indicated to us that they influence behavior in the same way that values do. Not much in the realm of sociology is ever set in stone. It's like learning to speak French, where the rules for conjugating a verb are always the same, except when they aren't.

7th	Loyalty	61%	*Loyalty* comes in various forms: to people, to places, to things, to processes, and to ideas. Sometimes it must be earned. Other times it's granted freely.
8th	Religion & Spirituality	58%	Formal or informal. Externalized or only for yourself. A meditation practice or walk in the woods might be your manifestation of this value, or you might be the pope.
9th	Employment Security	56%	If this is important to someone, they will prioritize activities that make their job more secure. This value often shows up with the other security values: *Financial Security* and plain ol' garden variety *Security*.
10th	Personal Responsibility	54%	These folks want to be the one who gets stuff done. They love saying yes.
11th	Basic Needs	54%	Regardless of income, some of us always have a nagging concern about paying the bills.
12th	Harmony	44%	Will pursue whatever helps achieve a sense of inner harmony.
13th	Health & Well-Being	44%	This means wildly different things: from being a triathlon junkie to not eating nacho chips on the sofa while watching Netflix.
14th	Experiences	43%	Let's do stuff! Some people want to do the same things over and over, and others are always hunting for a new thrill. Also, some like their experiences nearby, while others are willing to venture far away.
15th	Respect	42%	Treating others the way you wish to be treated.
16th	Compassion	41%	This has figured prominently in profiles of people in the medical profession and with police officers. Those in service-oriented professions score high for this, although others do, too.
17th	Social Standing	39%	How do other people see me in the hierarchies I'm part of? Am I seen as the wisest fisherman or the most astute collector of art?
18th	Creativity	39%	*Creativity* is in the eye of the beholder. We've seen creativity as an important value in what stereotypically might be considered the most uncreative groups of people—Wall Street quant investors, for example.

19th	Trustworthiness	38%	I can be relied on. I am the dependable one.
20th	Security	37%	One of three kinds of security, along with *Financial Security* and *Job Security*. They often show up together. When they do, it's a safe bet that the audience does not want any surprises in any part of their life. It shows up in the oddest places—for example, people who chase adventures all over the world often rank it highly.
21st	Education	37%	Some believe formal education is the path to greatness, and others simply enjoy learning so much that they are always looking to self-educate.
22nd	Tradition	35%	Older cultures have more of this, of course. But now we have stats to back it up. It can also relate to preservation of daily routines.
23rd	Balance	35%	We seem to talk about work-life balance more than we actually value it. This often can include other aspects of life, too.
24th	Love	34%	Almost always linked to something specific, like *Family*. Rarely appears without some sort of qualification (e.g., "My love for my kids…").
25th	Possessions	34%	Stuff. Doesn't have to be valuable but might be. The opposite of minimalism. At times linked to appearances: "I buy stuff so that others can see I have stuff."
26th	Patience	31%	Good things come to those who wait. *Patience* is a virtue. Pick your corny saying; these people follow it. They are likely accustomed to having their patience tested, or it wouldn't be on their radar as much as it is.
27th	Morality	30%	Thinking the right thoughts. Means different things to different people.
28th	Righteousness	30%	Doing the right things. Means different things to different people.
29th	Friendships	30%	One of several values that describe how we like to interact with the outside world. It's often seen as a subset of *Relationships*, which ranks in the number-two spot on this list, which may explain why this value is 29th.
30th	Authority	29%	They want it. And they like seeing it on display.

DAVID **ALLISON**

31st	Positive Environments	27%	Often a confusing one; this seems to be about avoiding bad things in all ways: mental, physical, spiritual, emotional. These people are negativity averse.
32nd	Happiness	27%	I'm sad this isn't higher up the list, but that's just me.
33rd	Ambition	26%	Often shows up alongside *Social Standing*.
34th	Self-Control	26%	The stoics of the world. They seek to control their emotions and actions, usually with one eye on some goal.
35th	Self-Expression	25%	Comfortable being in my own skin and being myself, whether you like it or not.
36th	Environmentalism	25%	This value shows up in at least two ways: those who are concerned with the environment that surrounds them and the ones they love and those who have a global view of the problems faced by planet Earth.
37th	Independence	24%	The freedom to be myself, make my own way, and make my own decisions.
38th	Wealth	24%	Not to be confused with *Money*, which is just about bank balances; *Wealth* is about a bigger picture. Perhaps this is an extreme version of *Financial Security*?
39th	Politeness	23%	Similar to *Respect* but also different. This can be about treating others the way you wish to be treated but also about being polite when faced with rudeness or unpleasant circumstances.
40th	Generosity	23%	Giving is better than receiving.
41st	Equality	23%	Recognition that everyone deserves an equal opportunity and access. It's less likely to be specific to individual things (e.g., food, housing); it's more general.
42nd	Service to Others	23%	This value relates to specific activities, tasks, and roles rather than a general attitude.
43rd	Dependability	22%	You can rely on me.
44th	Courage	19%	We often see this value when people have faced considerable challenges in their lives—they are conscious of the courage they have, or have had, to get through something difficult. That courage is then highly valued as a tool for the future.

45th	Cooperation	19%	To date, this is the only value of the 56 that has never ranked in the number-one spot. For anyone. In well over three-quarters of a million surveys.
46th	Tolerance	18%	We're all different; let's accept that. You be you.
47th	Leisure	18%	Despite how common it is to read/hear arguments in favor of work-life balance, this value scores curiously low.
48th	Influence	18%	A desire to be a leader and/or motivate others.
49th	Intimacy	17%	Specific to an individual relationship.
50th	Political Freedom	16%	A general sense of freedom, not so much about specific activities like voting.
51st	Peace	16%	Relates to life overall more than specific circumstances (e.g., "I want to live a peaceful life").
52nd	Money	15%	We see this appear with *Ambition* and *Social Standing* quite frequently but not always.
53rd	Unselfishness	15%	In the same family as *Respect* and *Politeness* but more about actions taken/not taken.
54th	Confidence	14%	Most see *Confidence* as a measure of growth and a doorway to other opportunities.
55th	Freedom of Speech	13%	It is usually attached to something big and important.
56th	Determination	9%	I have made up my mind to get this done, and by golly, it will get done!

Later in the book, in Part Four, I'm going to show you how you can harness these 56 values to engage and activate a target audience.

But first, in Part Three, I'm going to talk you through what values rank highest in each region of the world. Think of it as a drone flyover of the Valuegraphics Database—it's not super-duper granular, but it gives you a look at what is important in different parts of the world. This analysis matters for two reasons.

First, it's always fascinating to see what different people around the world care about. It shows us both how similar and how different we are.

Second, you need these chapters to begin reframing how you interpret the world. Remember how we said demographic thinking is ingrained in our DNA? Shaking it off isn't going to be easy, and you need practice. Part Three teaches you, little by little, how to look at the world through a valuegraphic lens and how to use something perhaps you didn't even know you had: your *sociological imagination.*

THIS IS WHAT WE CARE ABOUT ALL AROUND THE WORLD

CHAPTER 7

THE SOCIOLOGICAL IMAGINATION

THIS IS GOING TO BE FUN. WE ARE ABOUT TO EMBARK on a values-based tour of the world. We'll see what people in China value most of all and how they are different from people in Africa. We'll take a look at Americans and how they compare to Europeans. What do people in the Middle East have in common with folks who hail from Oceania? What makes Central/South America unique?

We've already explored the 56 values that drive everything humans do in Chapter 6 (if you need a refresher on those values, feel free to jump back to the chart there whenever you need). Now we'll see how these values cluster and rank for various parts of the world and lightly skim across a few things we've learned.

These chapters don't follow a standard formula. For some regions, I've chosen an interesting observation to talk about; for other places, I've highlighted a data disparity; in still other places, I've rambled on about a few things I hope you'll find interesting. Truth is, I've pretty much cherry-picked what I'll write about in these chapters because after 750,000 surveys, we've learned so much that I could write an entire book about each region.

So please understand the goal is not to tell you everything. The goal is to familiarize you with valuegraphic data and teach you a new skill. Unless you are a sociologist, this skill is likely a new way for you to think about data and the people in the world around you. And like any new skill, it takes practice to learn how to use it. I'm referring to using your sociological imagination.

WHAT IS THE SOCIOLOGICAL IMAGINATION?

There are a lot of definitions for the sociological imagination, but I like this one: the ability to form a picture of what's happening, or what might happen next, based on information you are presented with. Some sociologists will want to argue with me about that definition, but for our purposes as marketers and creators, it works great.

Sociological data comes with few hard-and-fast rules. The data itself is precise, but what the data means—how it is interpreted—can be colored by all sorts of outside influences. It's your job to look at the data, add as much other information as you have, and filter all that through your experiences and intuition to sort out what's going on. Here's an example.

The Yrjönkatu Swimming Hall is the first and oldest public indoor swimming hall in Finland. It was inaugurated on June 4, 1928.[11] Let's say we know for a fact, based on valuegraphic data, that something about the Yrjönkatu Swimming Hall in Helsinki is attracting tourists who place a very high value on *Social Standing*.

Using my sociological imagination, I could postulate that tourists are finding the *Social Standing* they value so highly because of the history of the building, the grand sweeping architecture, and the traditional saunas that are part of the experience. It all feels like the most Finnish way you could possibly swim, which gives tourists a great story to tell—about being an authentic traveler who goes where the locals go. This could boost their *Social Standing* when they get back home.

My hypothesis, courtesy of my sociological imagination, sounds plausible. But of course it is limited by what I know about tourists who swim at pools in Finland.

Now let's say the pool had a Director of Marketing named Tahira. When Tahira gets the valuegraphic data and discovers that *Social Standing* has such a huge influence on her tourist traffic, she uses her sociological imagination to develop a different theory. Tahira might agree that the *Social Standing* these folks crave comes from telling a story back home. But she'd know the story is not about Finnish

11   My Helsinki, "Yrjönkatu Swimming Hall," n.d., https://www.myhelsinki.fi/en/see-and-do/sights/yrj%C3%B6nkatu-swimming-hall

traditions so much as it is about one Finnish tradition in particular: swimming naked. You see, swimsuits were only *permitted* at the Yrjönkatu Swimming Hall after 2001, and most people still shy away from them.

Tahira and I both used our sociological imagination to answer the same question. We know the shared value that is bringing her target audience to this swimming pool is *Social Standing*, and we have ideas about why. Tahira had more context and experience to work with and came up with an answer that is more likely to be true. Tahira's next step should be to promote naked public swimming as the ultimate Finnish story to tell your friends back home.

Moreover, there's no need for her to waste time or money promoting the price of admission, the availability of free towels, or the parking arrangements because what her customers care about, what they value, is *Social Standing*. And what we value determines what we do.

Think of it this way. Valuegraphics Profiles are constructed with statistically accurate data but in many ways also resemble a work of art. A painting hanging on the wall in an art gallery is only a canvas with some marks on it until there's an audience, a viewer, to interact with it. The person looking at a painting—what they know, what they have seen, how they think about the world—is what creates meaning. So too with valuegraphic data. It only becomes meaningful when we wonder about it, and the answer will be different depending on who you are. *Valuegraphics are not the answer; they are the questions we must ask.* But they are the only questions that matter for any target audience because what we value determines everything we do. Valuegraphics focus all your energy and resources on the right mysteries.

In the following chapters, I'm going to take you on a value-based tour of the world, as promised, but I'm also going to show you how to use your sociological imagination to interpret valuegraphic data. This could mean leveraging your experience like Tahira did. Or it could mean collecting more knowledge about the context and environment. Or it could mean asking the right questions, or perhaps running speculative scenarios on what the data implies. There's no one right way to do this, no step-by-step strategy. Exactly like the imagination, the sociological imagination should be vast, unrestrained, and will work best when it can make surprising connections between disparate ideas.

So that's what I hope to show you in Part Three—how to use your sociological imagination to think about valuegraphic information. And I'm going to do that by using my own imagination to explore the data. You'll notice that these chapters are free-wheeling and open-ended, which is more or less the point. You must give yourself permission to ask questions, notice what you find interesting, and let your imagination run wild. For most people, this is a new way of thinking, and there's no right way to develop that skill.

CHAPTER 8

VALUEGRAPHICS OF THE WORLD

THE CHAPTERS IMMEDIATELY FOLLOWING THIS ONE WILL look at various regions of the world and point out some of the most interesting things we've uncovered. But let's begin with a look at the entire planet.

Looking at all 56 core human values for the entire world is an enormous task to kick off with, so let's warm up with the top three values on a simple map of the earth.

The first thing I would like to point out on this map is the disclaimer, which might seem like an odd place to start. It's crucial, though, because it waves a red flag about what this map does not include.

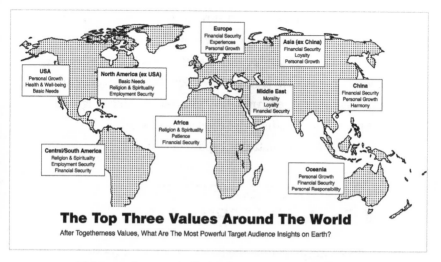

The Top Three Values Around The World

After Togetherness Values, What Are The Most Powerful Target Audience Insights on Earth?

This map does not include what we call the Togetherness Values. Why not? Let me explain.

There are five Togetherness Values. They are, in alphabetical order:

1. Belonging

2. Community

3. Family

4. Friendships

5. Relationships

The Togetherness Values are so dominant that they are all you'd see on this map of the world if we left them in. Almost without exception, they are the most important values everywhere on earth.

It's one of the most inspiring findings from all our research: what humans value more than anything else is being together. Every time I think about this, my heart fills with hope for the future. John Donne was right that "No man is an island,"[12] and I'm sure in these more PC times, he'd be OK with my updated version, "No one is an island."

If you look at the map, you will see several curious patterns. Looking for patterns is a great way to kick-start your sociological imagination. Keep in mind that even seeing something once is a pattern if everything else appears at least twice.

Here are a few patterns I spotted.

FINANCIAL SECURITY IS A GLOBAL CONCERN, ALMOST

Financial Security tops the list in Europe, China, and the rest of Asia, too, and gets an honorable mention in five other regions. Remember that *Financial Security* as a value does not indicate ongoing financial difficulties that need to be faced down. It only means that a sense of certainty about your financial situation is highly valued.

The only places where *Financial Security* does not appear in the top three are the United States and the rest of North America.[13] Which begs the question, what is it about North Americans overall that bucks the *Financial Security* trend? If your organization operates in various regions of the world, your target audience in North America will not be as influenced by *Financial Security* compared to people who live anywhere else on earth.

However, for most of the world, appealing to *Financial*

---

12 John Donne, "Devotions Upon Emergent Occasions and Seuerall Steps in my Sicknes – Meditation XVII," 1623, https://www.theidioms.com/no-man-is-an-island/

13 People are often surprised to learn that North America actually includes 23 sovereign nations. As well as the United States, the remaining 22 nations that make up North America include Antigua and Barbuda, Bahamas, Barbados, Belize, Canada, Costa Rica, Cuba, Dominica, Dominican Republic, El Salvador, Grenada, Guatemala, Haiti, Honduras, Jamaica, Mexico, Nicaragua, Saint Kitts and Nevis, Panama, Saint Lucia, Saint Vincent and the Grenadines, and Trinidad and Tobago.

Security could help you engage and activate your audience in many different ways.

- Monthly payment plans, with an option to pause payments should the need arise, would appeal to those who value Financial Security.

- Calculating and highlighting the potential savings that a product or service would trigger ("this thing will pay for itself in X years!") is another straightforward way to tell a Financial Security story.

- When a university admission program sells undergraduate admissions by pointing to wealthy alumni who've leveraged a degree into a lifetime of success, that's the value of *Financial Security* on parade.

It would be fascinating to see which brands in which parts of the world focus on *Financial Security* and how that compares to valuegraphic data. Maybe someone searching for a PhD topic will read this and be keen to give it a go. Feel free to reach out if that's you: we can give you the ranking for *Financial Security* in 180 countries. That's a good place to start!

BASIC NEEDS IS A TOP CONCERN ONLY IN NORTH AMERICA

This might be the light bulb moment that illuminates the previous point about *Financial Security*.

Basic Needs shows up on the map for only the United States and for the rest of North America.

Could this be a nomenclature issue? Maybe respondents in North America who indicated *Basic Needs* was an important value in their lives meant the same thing as respondents from other parts of the world who chose *Financial Security*?

My gut tells me that people focused on *Financial Security* want to preserve a positive state of security, whereas the *Basic Needs* camp actively avoids a negative state of debt and default.

For those of you who want to see how the 56 values rank if we include the Togetherness Values, this next map is for you. Note how similar each region becomes. We aren't all that different from each other anywhere on earth. And just so you know, from this point forward, I'll leave the Togetherness Values in the charts you see in this book.

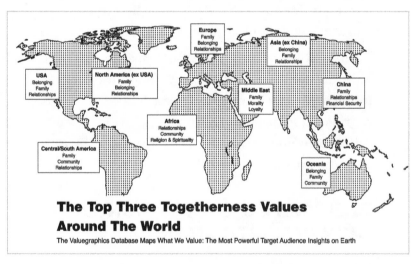

The Top Three Togetherness Values Around The World

The Valuegraphics Database Maps What We Value: The Most Powerful Target Audience Insights on Earth

ANOTHER PERSPECTIVE ON GLOBAL VALUES

The chart above shows all 56 core human values ranked in order of importance for the population of planet Earth. This ranking was compiled from our nearly 750,000 surveys in 152 languages across 180 countries.

When I sit back and look at this macro-visualization, the product of all the work that's been done on the Valuegraphics Database over the last five years, it's a bit overwhelming. You are looking at the most complex record of what humans care about that has ever been created. It makes me stop and think about the global challenges we face today.

As I write this, the world is reeling from the effects of a global pandemic. The environmental security of our planet is under critical threat on countless fronts. Populations are at war. Genocides still happen. Migrants flee unbearable conditions and are met with hatred and violence. Entire economies are hanging by a thread. New fault lines continue to emerge that further delineate us versus them. There are enormous numbers of people on this planet who do not have clean drinking water or sufficient food, while there are others with a fleet of private jets (even rocket ships!) on standby. So many people still fight for equality: there are places in the world where you can be executed for being gay, where the color of your skin makes you a second-class citizen, where your gender dictates what you can and can't do.

But what if the whole world, on every level, was guided by a factual understanding of our core human values? Not a random and ever-changing interpretation of values that politicians and lobbyists use to justify their political ideologies but a unifying set of core human values based on data and science?

In my dream world, this chart of global values would become a guiding light for global leaders. They would use

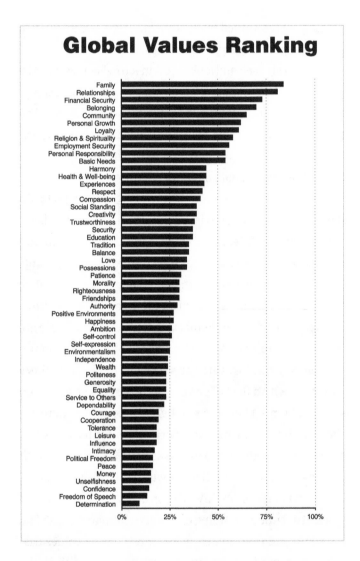

Global Values Ranking

it to make decisions about what to prioritize. I've often day-dreamed how much of a game changer it would be if elected leaders globally, nationally, regionally, and right down to the level of cities and towns were given the valuegraphics for the people they represent and then held to account for how well they respond to what their constituents truly care about.

It's not a likely scenario, I admit. And I am sure there are philosophical flaws in this big grand dream of mine. But regardless, let's play a game.

If you and I were elected the leaders of the entire world and we had the global values chart to work from, what would we do? To make things a bit easier, here are the top 10 values for the world, plus the Togetherness Values that make the cut.

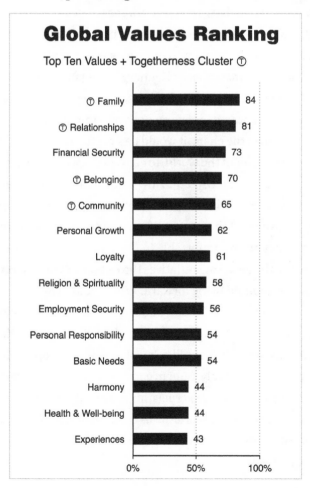

Global Values Ranking

Top Ten Values + Togetherness Cluster ⓣ

Value	Score
ⓣ Family	84
ⓣ Relationships	81
Financial Security	73
ⓣ Belonging	70
ⓣ Community	65
Personal Growth	62
Loyalty	61
Religion & Spirituality	58
Employment Security	56
Personal Responsibility	54
Basic Needs	54
Harmony	44
Health & Well-being	44
Experiences	43

Based on these valuegraphics, the first thing I would do as leader of the world is find ways to strengthen and protect families. But I'd never leave that word hanging out there like a single piece of laundry drying on a line. *Family* means so many things to so many people, and all the definitions are valid and beautiful. My idea of *Family* might be more about my chosen family, and it may or may not include my biological family. It could also mean a family with two moms and two dads and an auntie, or whatever, and that's OK as well. For some people, it might be a small nucleus. For others, it might be an entire glorious ecosystem of people they love. The metaphorical laundry line is jam-packed with fresh linens and towels and sheets, and they are all happily flapping in a warm breeze on a sunny summer day.

Based on the chart, it would be a perfectly supportable move, as leader of the world, to convene a special task force to study *Personal Growth*. How can we help the citizens of the world feel like they are moving forward, improving themselves and their lot in life, learning new things, and becoming more comfortable in their own skin? I'd love to listen to the amazing initiatives the *Personal Growth* global task force would bring forward. Who wouldn't?

Financial Security can't be neglected. With so much economic disparity in the world and varying ideas of what *Financial Security* looks like, it would not be a simple value to augment equitably. But I'm convinced it would be worth enduring endless and excruciating conversations about economic theory. Because if citizens could all find the *Financial Security* they seek, there'd be fewer fights and disputes around the world.

There are so many things to think about. What would happen if we combined our overwhelming desire for *Belonging* with the importance we place on *Health & Well-Being*? What if our shared values around *Relationships* and *Loyalty* were harnessed in ways that made the world a better place? We can keep going, imagining how to give people more of what they care about. But the truth is, you and I are probably not going to have the chance to implement these ideas on a global scale.

But we can chip away at this. There are more than 115 million companies in the world. If even a small percentage stopped using divisive demographic stereotypes to understand their target audiences and instead embraced the unifying values that we share as humans, it would be a great start. One organization at a time, we can get to a better place in a better way.

CHAPTER 9

THE VALUEGRAPHICS OF THE UNITED STATES

IN THE UNITED STATES, PEOPLE PLACE THE HIGHEST VALUE on fitting in, or *Belonging*, followed by *Family*, and then *Relationships*, the other people they know. Americans are a chummy bunch.

And they are driven, too. Up in fourth place, we see *Personal Growth*, the desire to be better versions of themselves, almost neck and neck with *Health & Well-Being*. Not surprisingly, they also want to make sure the bills get paid and their necessities are taken care of (*Basic Needs*)

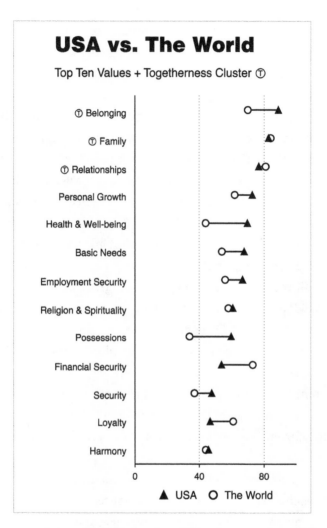

USA vs. The World

Top Ten Values + Togetherness Cluster ⓣ

	USA	The World
ⓣ Belonging		
ⓣ Family		
ⓣ Relationships		
Personal Growth		
Health & Well-being		
Basic Needs		
Employment Security		
Religion & Spirituality		
Possessions		
Financial Security		
Security		
Loyalty		
Harmony		

0   40   80

▲ USA   O The World

by remaining gainfully employed (*Employment Security*).

God or yoga comes next (*Religion & Spirituality*). After that, it's time to think about the stuff they have and the stuff they want to buy next (*Possessions*), plus ensuring they have the means to do it (*Financial Security*).

If we continue down the list of the top 10 values, we

quickly fall off the 50th percentile precipice—the remaining values on the chart are important to half of the population, give or take. So we will stop short of that milestone and look at what we've already learned.

If you are a citizen of the United States reading this book, this recital of the most VIP American values may not seem like much of a revelation. And that's more or less the point. This list of the values of your nation will feel logical and normal to you because these are very likely to be your most VIP values, too.

But let's look past the surface and imagine how these insights might get put to use.

If you are looking to engage and activate Americans, it would be more powerful to talk about ways to grow and improve than it would be to focus on the basic necessities of life.

If you have a company that sells online courses to help people learn new job skills, it will be more successful if you point to the *Personal Growth* that continuing education provides instead of the potential for a better-paying job to help pay the rent because *Personal Growth* is more VIP than *Basic Needs.*

Of course, combining messages about both *Personal Growth* and *Basic Needs* will be more successful still. Throw in some obvious connection to how your course offerings will help your graduates make things better for their *Family* and maybe even help them fit in with their peer group (*Belonging, Relationships*), and I'll give you a gold star. Further, you'll be an expert at valuegraphics if you can figure out how to connect your message to the values of *Possessions* and *Religion & Spirituality* as well.

A couple of points to remember:

As we only ever do things or feel a certain way because of a value, this list of values for the entire population of the United States is like a secret code you can use to engage Americans. There are 56 possible values that humans use to navigate life, but in the United States, you can more or less ignore anything not on this list because these particular values are shared by the largest swaths of the American population. Of course, that's assuming your target audience is the entire population of the United States, which is highly unlikely.

More likely is that your target audience is Americans who collect teacups, Americans who take vitamins, or Americans who love cashmere sweaters. For each of those groups, some entirely different values would rise to the top of the list. The values that lead to teacup obsession, for example, will not be shared by the entire nation.

Think of it this way.

We could describe the ideal conditions required to grow apples—the kind of soil, the nutrients that produce the best results. How much water, shade and sunshine are optimal. What other species of tree can be nearby and share the same patch of earth and which ones should be banned from being in the same garden plot.

But if you are growing pink pearl apples or knobbed russet apples, the best practices will vary. In fact, they could vary considerably. If you want your particular apple to win the ribbon at the state fair, you will want to know the specific deviations from the norm that will produce the most amazing results.

COMPARING VALUES—
WHAT ELSE CAN WE LEARN?

If you've picked up this book to learn how to engage your target audience and you live and work in the United States, there's some danger in thinking that what feels normal and obvious to you is some kind of universal truth. It's helpful to compare values with another set of data as a kind of reality check. The chart at the beginning of this chapter (and the chapters that follow) uses the global values ranking as a comparative set.

The number-one value in America, *Belonging*, is less important in the rest of the world. In fact, the United States is part of a minority group of three regions where *Belonging* is in the top spot. Asia (excluding China) and Oceania are also part of this exclusive club.

As *Belonging* is not the most important value for vast areas of the world, it would be a huge mistake to assume that creating messages or positioning along the lines of "We are all in this together" would be a global success. I tend toward exaggeration when I am trying to make a point, and this is one of those instances. Clearly, *Belonging* is still an important value in all regions of the world, but it's not the gold medal winner of the values race that you might expect if you rely solely on an American perspective.

As a Canadian, I've traveled through life alongside the American people by virtue of geography. Plus, I went to college in the United States, where I witnessed this ultra-dominant desire to belong firsthand. This is my own limited perspective, of course, but I've always suspected that the drive to be part of a bigger picture, to belong to a movement, to see life as tribal, is more pronounced on the American side of the 49th parallel. I think the stat we've unearthed with our research—that *Belonging* sits at the pinnacle of the values chart for America—is proof that my hunch is correct.

To be clear, I'm not being judgmental about this. To quote the Bard, "There is nothing either good or bad, but thinking makes it so." I'm using my sociological imagination to look at the world. I hope by the time you are finished reading this book, you will fall into this same habit, too.

Let's zip over to another region of the world now and see what else the Valuegraphics Database has uncovered. It's time to talk about Europe.

CHAPTER 10

THE VALUEGRAPHICS OF THE EUROPEAN UNION

IN EUROPE, AS IN MANY OTHER PARTS OF THE WORLD, *Family* comes first. *Belonging* comes a close second and *Relationships* is squished up at the top of the chart, too.

Something interesting to note: look how closely the three Togetherness Values rank to each other. They are only a point or two apart, which, if you allow for the +/−3.5% margin of error in our data, means you could justifiably statethat all three values are of equal importance.

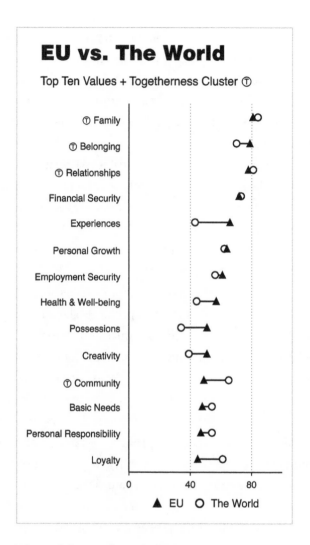

EU vs. The World

Top Ten Values + Togetherness Cluster Ⓣ

Ⓣ Family	
Ⓣ Belonging	
Ⓣ Relationships	
Financial Security	
Experiences	
Personal Growth	
Employment Security	
Health & Well-being	
Possessions	
Creativity	
Ⓣ Community	
Basic Needs	
Personal Responsibility	
Loyalty	

0   40   80

▲ EU   O The World

What might you do with this?

Let's say you are an accounting firm operating in a handful of European Union (EU) countries and working to position your brand in the most engaging way possible. The interchangeable importance of *Family*, *Belonging*, and *Relationships* might convince you to use a personal and human biography for each partner on your company website. What do the leaders of your firm like to do with their friends when they are not at work? What does family time look like for them? What can you share about your partners that would signal to potential clients that they will fit in and belong?

How could you reinforce these values with your current clients to keep them magnetically attached to your firm? What thought leadership could you orchestrate, what social media assets could you create, what new tools and online resources could you provide that would make your brand approachable and welcoming?

It seems to me that most accounting firms are running in the opposite direction, talking primarily about how their smart partners do smart things in smart ways. What would it look like if you were the only firm to stake a claim around the values of *Belonging*, *Relationships*, and *Family*? You'd certainly attract a lot of attention, and isn't that the name of the game?

Of course, if your brand has already staked a claim based on complex credentials and professional expertise, then your current clients have been attracted to you because those cues are activating a set of values they share. It may be best to stay the course. Even so, adding a little bit of huggability wouldn't hurt, based on what this European values chart suggests.

As you might imagine, we'd all be fast asleep if I rambled on about every single value on these regional charts, so I'm focusing on only a few in each case. Please don't take that to mean that the other values on the chart are somehow less intriguing or applicable. In fact, one or two of the untouched values might be the most important insights for your particular set of circumstances.

CREATIVITY MAKES THE CUT

I feel energized whenever I see *Creativity* show up for any target audience. A little voice deep in the recesses of my brain screams, "David, these are your people!" So it's exponentially exciting when *Creativity* shows up in the top 10 list for an *entire region of the world.* Perhaps this is why I like spending time in Europe so much.

Since I'm such a fan of this particular value, here's a bonus chart that shows how *Creativity* shows up around the world. Look at Europe at the top, basking in the *Creativity* sunshine. I need no further validation for the comfort I derive from Europe's confusing streets, complicated sauces, and innate elegance.

When we look at a single value like this, remember there are 56 values in total. Our database identifies which ones rise to the top for any audience we are profiling, *but that does not mean those folks dislike the other values.* In other words, although *Creativity* is ranked 32nd in Africa, it only means there are 24 other values that are more important in Africa. It does not mean that my African friends and colleagues are creativity haters.

This is an important distinction on any Valuegraphics Profile for any group of people. There are no losers. All the values are important, but some are more important than others. And if you get any Orwellian *Animal Farm* vibes from that last sentence, please disregard.

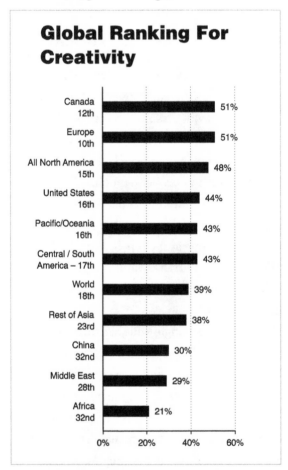

Global Ranking For Creativity

Canada 12th	51%
Europe 10th	51%
All North America 15th	48%
United States 16th	44%
Pacific/Oceania 16th	43%
Central / South America – 17th	43%
World 18th	39%
Rest of Asia 23rd	38%
China 32nd	30%
Middle East 28th	29%
Africa 32nd	21%

EXPERIENCES AND POSSESSIONS BOTH MATTER

It's unusual to see both *Experiences* and *Possessions* score high in a Valuegraphics Profile. Normally, one or the other pops up but rarely both. In fact, I can't think of a single instance when both have appeared in the top 10 for a custom Valuegraphics Profile for any client, except when one of these values engulfs the other. For example, we have seen target audiences where *Experiences* are considered *Possessions*.

This comingling of values helps explain my obsession with uncommon hotels. When traveling, I'll save money in other ways so I can splurge on the most interesting hotel. Chateau Marmont in Hollywood is a great example. It's expensive. It's a bit tattered, and it certainly doesn't try hard to be luxurious. But you can feel the ghosts of John Belushi and Helmut Newton, both of whom died there, brushing past you in the hallway. Spending a week there was technically an experience for me, but to this day, the memory of my stay feels like a possession.

We have also seen target audiences where the inverse is true, and *Possessions* are thought of as *Experiences*.

On one of my first trips to Paris decades ago with the love of my life, we wandered into a terribly exclusive art gallery in a chic part of town. We were starting out as art collectors and had purchased a few inexpensive works of art back home—enough to be full of misplaced bravado. We said the right things, asked the right questions, and earned ourselves a wonderful hour with an impossibly Parisienne woman from the gallery. She had flawless English, perfect hair, and an unstudied elegance that I can remember to this day. She validated everything we said and had us convinced we were the smartest art collectors she'd ever met. She was a masterful sales professional!

Then it came time to commit to buying a tiny sculpture we'd been talking about for the last hour. When she told us the price, we had to work hard not to pass out in front of our new friend. We gulped, paid up, and ate ramen for a month to make up for it.

We still have that sculpture, and it's a great example of the value we place on *Possessions*. But far more importantly, the *experience of acquiring it* was and is a foundationally significant moment in our lifelong love affair.

All of which is to say, if you are working on a brand in the EU, ask yourself how this dichotomy of values might come into play. Could your offering be a tangible object that is an experience? Or is it an experience disguised as a tangible artifact? If it isn't one or the other already, is there some way you could create that duality?

I can't leave this topic without telling you about a remarkable store in Berlin called Manufactum (www.manufactum.com). They have created the ever-elusive, much-discussed "retail experience" that ensures any purchase you make is secondary to the act of having been there. In fact, while writing this, I reached out to a friend who was with me on my last visit, and we reminisced about how cool, useful, and fun this store is. I have no idea what I bought there. Neither does he. But we possess the shared memory of that experience together.

And just now, I spent a glorious hour on the Manufactum website. Although it's nowhere near as impactful as being there in the flesh, it does a remarkable job by harnessing every nuance possible: the fonts, the practical but beautiful layout and UX, and the curious and insanely useful selection of things you definitely need. I bookmarked the page and made a mental note to go back and buy various twines, Opinel knives, and the goat hair radiator brush I suddenly can't imagine living without despite not having any radiators. I felt sad to leave—sad to leave a freakin' online store! How did they do that to me? They've created a remarkable experience. Gold stars all around.

CONFIDENCE IS MUCH MORE DOMINANT

Survey respondents in the EU ranked the value of *Confidence* twice as high as anywhere else in the world! This is worth paying attention to.

According to Wikipedia, "Confidence is a state of being clear-headed either that a hypothesis or prediction is correct or that a chosen course of action is the best or most effective."

Now, some survey respondents were reacting more to the notion of self-confidence specifically, instead of confidence generally. *Confidence* comes from a Latin word *fidere*, which means "to trust." Therefore, having self-confidence is having trust in oneself. One's self-confidence increases from experiences of having satisfactorily completed particular activities. It is a positive belief that in the future, one can generally accomplish what one wishes to do.[14]

To help give this conversation some additional context, here is how *Confidence* ranks across all regions of the world.

---

14 Wikipedia, "Confidence," April 16, 2022, https://en.wikipedia.org/wiki/Confidence

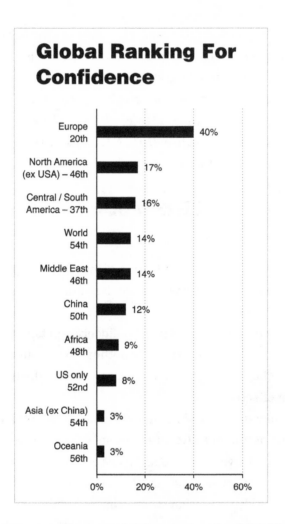

Global Ranking For Confidence

Europe — 20th	40%
North America (ex USA) — 46th	17%
Central / South America — 37th	16%
World — 54th	14%
Middle East — 46th	14%
China — 50th	12%
Africa — 48th	9%
US only — 52nd	8%
Asia (ex China) — 54th	3%
Oceania — 56th	3%

How can we account for the oversupply of *Confidence* in Europe? I wonder if the centuries-long dominance of European culture over a significant part of the world has contributed to the situation. Perhaps it gave rise to a sense of self-confidence among Europeans, who would then naturally and circuitously find the value of *Confidence* more important than others would.

Is the ability to stride comfortably through a familiar world a confidence booster, and as a result, is *Confidence* more highly valued? Do we value what we see in the mirror when we self-evaluate? Is this some kind of macro confirmation bias?

Nevertheless and regardless of the reasons, it's our task to use this highly ranked value to engage and influence when faced with a European target audience.

It seems to me that the opposite of *Confidence* might be timidity. The world is full of timid products, services, and brands that try hard to be all things to all people. Unfortunately, they end up being nothing to anyone.

But now that we see how much importance is placed on *Confidence* by consumers in the EU, organizations should feel emboldened. It's statistically supportable to take a stand and plant a flag in the consumer mindscape. Brands can go about being the most extreme version of themselves, exuding *Confidence* with every step they take.

RELIGION & SPIRITUALITY SCORES LOW

I learned this a long time ago: if you want to stay friends with people, don't talk about religion or politics. And I consider all of you to be my friends. But I will throw out one cautionary note for those of you who want to consider this data point more fulsomely.

Remember that there are all kinds of religions, and everyone will have a different idea of what spirituality means to them. A regular yoga class, a quiet walk in an old-growth forest, a meditation practice, or faithful attendance at an orthodox service—all are manifestations of the value of *Religion & Spirituality*. Given the relatively low importance placed on this value, you might want to pause and have a good think before leaning in too heavily in the European marketplace.

CHAPTER 11

THE VALUEGRAPHICS OF CHINA

CHINA IS A REMARKABLY UNIQUE PLACE, VALUEGRAPHically speaking. Besides what you can see on the chart, there are macro-patterns in the database that appear only in this region of the world. Let me try to explain.

First, people in China have a far broader spectrum of definitions for values. It's more like a region of many countries, like Europe, where we see a systemic diversity that results from various cultures and countries grouped together as one.

Here's an example. Although 65% of the population in China agrees that *Loyalty* is important in their lives, what they mean by that varies wildly. If you ask 100 people from a country to define *Loyalty*, you will get many definitions. In China, however, you will get many more.

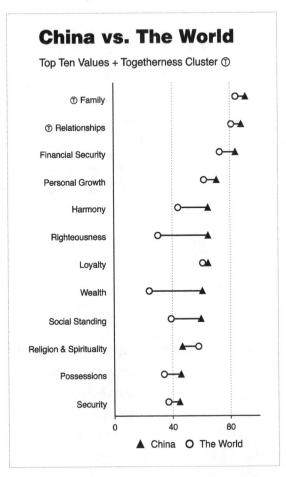

China vs. The World

Top Ten Values + Togetherness Cluster ⓣ

This ability to incorporate great diversity of opinion is in line with overarching ideas about Chinese culture and traditional values. After a few weeks of reading, which is admittedly only a quick skim across the surface of what's available, I noted an underlying and unifying belief that harmony more or less requires diversity. Put another way, balancing many things creates a stronger unified whole. I'm doing my best to summarize centuries of philosophical thought, and I'm butchering it, so let's hear from an expert.

In her article "China's Traditional Cultural Values and National Identity," Zhang Lihua, a resident scholar at the Carnegie—Tsinghua Center for Global Policy and a professor at the Department of International Relations at Tsinghua University, explained it this way:

> According to the concept of harmony, the universe unites diversity. Difference does not necessarily equal contradiction. Differences sometimes evolve into contradictions, but sometimes they constitute a necessary condition for harmony. There are many examples in which differences complement each other in nature and society. Uniting diversity is the basis for the generation of new things. Confucius said, "The gentleman aims at harmony, and not at uniformity (junzi he er bu tong, 君子和而不同)." Thus, a gentleman may hold different views, but he does not blindly follow others. Instead, he seeks to coexist harmoniously with them.[15]

A harmonious diversity is not an easy thing for my North American brain to grab hold of. But the responses from our survey participants certainly illustrate that many paths can lead to the same destination. Is it a coincidence that the most prominent hall in the Forbidden City, with a full complement of 10 different animal statues on each roof ridge, is called the Hall of Supreme Harmony?[16]

15 Zhang Lihua, "China's Traditional Cultural Values and National Identity," Nov. 21, 2013, https://carnegieendowment.org/2013/11/21/china-s-traditional-cultural-values-and-national-identity-pub-53613

16 Travel China Guide, "Mysterious Animals on the Palace Roofs of the Forbidden City," Nov. 11, 2022, https://www.travelchinaguide.com/attraction/beijing/forbidden-city/animals-on-the-palace-roofs.htm

Another fascinating anomaly in the data for China has to do with the value of *Family*. Even though *Family* tops the list of values in many parts of the world, the blunt dominance of this value in China would be hard to overstate. *Family* is an ultra-super-mega-value in China.

It's not a subtle thing; it's blatant and obvious, like certain married people who dress alike and hold hands in public...even from a distance, across a crowded room, it's clear that these people are married. *Family* is even the driver behind other values in ways we rarely see in other parts of the world.

There's another *Family* pattern in the Chinese data that I call the square-dancing paradigm.

In square dancing, four couples face each other in a square, and once the music starts, all sorts of things can happen. You can bow to your partner, promenade, swing someone around in a circle, or do something called an allemande. But regardless of what happens while the music plays, you always end up back where you started.

That's more or less how the value of *Family* works in China. For the vast majority of the population, it's the starting point for everything, and no other values come into play until *Family* is satisfied. Once you feel that you've got things all sorted out for your *Family*, you can go off and chase other values, metaphorically square dancing all over the place. But you will snap right back to where you started, refocused on *Family*, if something comes along to knock things off kilter.

Let's say you find out your grandpa has shuffled off the big dance floor of life, and your widowed grandma is beside herself with grief. You will abandon all other values and focus on *Family* until things stabilize, at which point you can resume dancing with the other values in your own personal valuegraphic profile.

HOW DOES ALL THIS IMPACT THE WAY YOU TARGET AN AUDIENCE IN CHINA?

Two things to keep in mind.

First, as you look at the values for China, keep in mind the vast diversity of meanings behind each value. Pull out all the stops as you work to understand how a value, or a group of values, will impact the work you have to do. Think broadly.

The incredible diversity of meaning ascribed to various values creates possible nuances that can only be understood in the context of a specific question. In other words, the most logical way to interpret what *Loyalty* means to a target audience will be clearer to you than to me because I don't know if you are trying to sell flip-flops, Ferraris, or firewood. It's a valuegraphic rainbow of possibilities.

Second, as a marketer, you must keep the absolute dominance of *Family* top of mind. You'd be certifiable if you didn't. It's crucial. Furthermore, because *Family* is hardwired to other values, everything that impacts *Family* will have a cascading impact on everything else. Since so many things can impact *Family* and the values attached to it, this quickly turns into a game of Jenga. One change can destabilize or even upend the whole thing. Leveraging the power of *Family* with a target audience in China will be enormously influential if you can harness it and extremely dangerous if you don't get it right.

A closing observation, made with my sociological imagination running in high gear. I see one group of values that feel related to each other: *Wealth*, *Social Standing*, and *Financial Security*. Let's call these the Doing Well values. And there's another trio made up of *Loyalty*, *Righteousness*, and *Harmony* that we could nickname the Doing It Right values.

In China, it could be argued there is an enormous importance placed on simultaneously Doing Well and Doing It Right. And you know what? Although it's dangerously anecdotal, I have many Chinese friends, and this sums up what I love about them quite nicely.

CHAPTER 12

THE VALUEGRAPHICS OF AFRICA

I HAVE A CONFESSION TO MAKE. WRITING A CHAPTER ABOUT the valuegraphics of an entire region of the world is a tiny bit intimidating. Don't get me wrong; it's fascinating and fun. But there is a weighty obligation to keep my Western perspective in check and look at what we've found with the wide-open eyes of a child.

It helps to remind myself that I'm only writing these chapters to show you various ways to interpret valuegraphic data. These chapters are the first few words—not the final word—on what the data means in each region. I hope my narratives convince you to bring your own thoughts to the table.

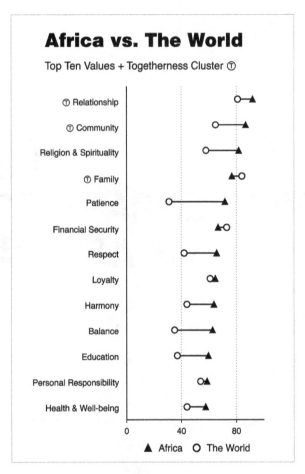

Africa vs. The World

Top Ten Values + Togetherness Cluster ⑦

	Africa ▲	The World ○
⑦ Relationship		
⑦ Community		
Religion & Spirituality		
⑦ Family		
Patience		
Financial Security		
Respect		
Loyalty		
Harmony		
Balance		
Education		
Personal Responsibility		
Health & Well-being		

0   40   80

▲ Africa   ○ The World

As we said in Chapter 7, how you interpret valuegraphic data is crucial. Remember Yrjönkatu Swimming Hall and the different conclusions Tahira and I reached? One way to understand valuegraphic data or a Valuegraphics Profile is to find people who know more than you do about the subject and look to them for context. You still need to connect the dots to your own circumstances, but context makes it easier.

Back in my old real estate marketing days, we'd often

be working on a big resort project in an unfamiliar (and usually tropical) part of the world. We'd attend an on-site meeting with a team of consultants to help us "interpret the location" or understand the "sense of place." The best of these meetings always had some locals involved—people who could explain what was special and unique about a place based on a lifetime of experience.

So that's what I've done in this chapter. I've found some secondary research and writings by other people and had some fascinating conversations, too.[17]

I started my deep dive by going on a Google binge, and I found a lot to read by people who know what they are talking about. It's interesting that five values show up in the Valuegraphics Database as more important in Africa than in any other region of the world: *Relationships*, *Community*, *Religion & Spirituality*, *Patience*, and *Balance*. In fact, I found an enormous amount of writing specifically about these five values. Not that I had any doubts, but real-world reassurances of our methodological accuracy are always a feel-good moment!

RELATIONSHIPS AND COMMUNITY

Macaulay A. Kanu, in his article "The Indispensability of the Basic Social Values in African Tradition: A Philosophical Appraisal," explains the value of *Relationships* in Africa:

> "Everyone is mindful that each person has something to contribute to his welfare, no matter the degree."

Later, in the same article, he references *Community*:

---

17 Special thanks to Nankhonde Kasonde-van den Broek, Founder and Chief Executive Officer at Zanga African Metrics, and Tes Proos, President at SITE Africa.

"The authentic African is known and identified in, by, and through his community. In the economic sphere, the guiding principle for the economic arrangement is that of being one's brother's keeper or caring for each other's welfare, at least within one's immediate community. The basic principle of the African social structure is communalism."[18]

For me, those two values, *Relationships* and *Community*, when looked at through Kanu's lens, are intensely reciprocal. Everyone knows that they are responsible for and to each other. As a marketer, this would have profound implications.

Nankhonde Kasonde-van den Broek, Founder and Chief Executive Officer at Zanga African Metrics, brought this up in a discussion we had about the concept of Ubuntu. In her words, Ubuntu translates as "I am because you are, and you are because I am." A philosophical cliché that often gets thrown around in the West is the question, "Am I my brother's keeper?" In Africa, the answer is unequivocally yes.

This made me think of all the products, services, and brands that position themselves by repositioning something else. Creating a sense of "other" is a time-honored tradition in cutthroat and competitive Western marketing. The valuegraphics for Africa might suggest emphasizing the intertwined nature of all things instead.

Could "those other guys aren't anywhere near as good as us" be replaced with "some people will prefer this over that"? Here are a few examples that illustrate a typically Western repositioning of the competition. I wonder if they would fly in Africa.

18　Macaulay A. Kanu, "The Indispensability of the Basic Social Values in African Tradition: A Philosophical Appraisal," GIRISI: A New Journal of African Studies 7, no. 1 (August 2010): 149–161, https://www.ajol.info/index.php/og/article/view/57930/46296

- Scope mouthwash repositioned Listerine, without naming them, by letting people know that Scope doesn't leave you with "medicine breath."

- Avis Car Rental famously quipped, "We're number 2, so we try harder," which of course implies that the other guys are slackers.

- The Apple computer campaign "I'm a Mac and I'm a PC" featured a boring and uptight dude in a gray suit as a PC user, while the Apple enthusiast was a cool, laid-back character. It's a funny construct, but is it as motivating in Africa as it is in the United States?

I'm not sure if these campaigns ran in Africa and, if they did, what the results were. I'm just throwing it out there. Given the uniquely interdependent importance of *Community* and *Relationships*, I wonder if a less divisive, more inclusive African approach would have been more successful. If you are doing business in Africa or plan to, it's worth considering.

RELIGION & SPIRITUALITY

Depending on who you ask, *Religion & Spirituality* is a value that can be powerful for marketers or dangerous. It never fails to elicit opinions one way or another. I argue for a larger definition that can be unifying for both camps, and the valuegraphics for Africa seem to back me up.

In his article "Locating African Values in 21st Century Economics," Onuoha Frank wrote,

> "To the African, religion is sine qua non; it is indispens-
> able. In fact, some scholars describe the average African
> as 'incurably religious.' Religion defines his perspec-
> tive on the world order; there is no 'being' without a
> 'Supreme Being.'"[19]

Kasonde-van den Broek had a slightly different way of talking about it. She told me that regardless of the spiritual path, denomination, or system you believe in, the idea that you are part of something bigger than yourself is vital to keeping the collective nature of society together. *Religion & Spirituality*, she explained, binds everyone to everyone else and provides rules to live by so the system stays strong.

When it shows up in a Valuegraphics Profile, *Religion & Spirituality* can mean full-on orthodoxy with all its pageantry and hardline dogma, but it can also simply refer to an awareness of spirit as part of the human condition.

Here's an example from my own life.

I'm self-aware enough to realize that most things I tackle with an all-or-nothing mentality. When I turned my attention to yoga several years ago, it was no different. I sought out a specific yoga teacher who I had heard great things about and convinced him to do 10 private sessions with me. This was a necessary first step so I could gain a competitive advantage...I had to win at yoga.

But for me, despite what many will see as my misaligned combativeness, yoga was still a spiritual endeavor. I was there because of the value I place on *Religion & Spirituality* in my own messed-up way.

The reason I'm telling you this story is to point out that

---

19 Onuoha Frank, "Locating African Values in 21st Century Economics," African Liberty: Latest Issues in Africa, September 19, 2015, https://www.africanliberty.org/2015/09/09/onuoha-frank-locating-african-values-in-twenty-first-century-economics/

Religion & Spirituality, like all values, must be seen through the eyes of your target audience. If you keep that in mind, this value can be intensely powerful. Even though I was there to dominate the game and become MVP, during my yoga days, you would have been able to sell me Tibetan singing bowls, mandala-etched yoga mats, sitar music libraries, and all sorts of other yoga paraphernalia by pointing out how it would connect me to something bigger.

PATIENCE

Africa is the only place in the world where *Patience* makes the top 10 list of most important values. If we are going to explore what this value is about, this is the place to do it.

For marketers, the implications of *Patience* as a component part of the operating system for the African market are profound. It is directly connected to the concept of time. Even the most cursory Google search for "Africa + Patience" leads to a string of articles by wide-eyed Westerners working or living in Africa for the first time. These authors are united in their initial overheated frustration and eventual chill acceptance of the fluidity of time in Africa. People are late. Or they simply don't show up. Or they show up at some other time than initially scheduled.

Kasonde-van den Broek suggested a different perspective on *Patience*. She pointed out how everything has a season, and things happen at the right time for the right reason.

Conversely, I'm noticing more emphasis on time in my hyper-Westernized life. Time is a precious resource, I'm told repeatedly, and I should think about time blocking, time sharing, time scarcity, and how, if I focus on the allocation of minutes instead of hours, I will maximize my time efficiency.

What's more, companies aggressively insist that I pay attention to time-limited offers, complete an online form in the next five minutes, use the password they emailed me within the next 10 minutes, download something before it expires in 48 hours, visit their store for this-weekend-only special discounts, and remember to return any merchandise I am unhappy with in two weeks or less.

Consequently, I feel I've become the rabbit from *Alice in Wonderland*, with the enormous pocket watch, dashing around spouting his famous line, "I'm late! I'm late! For a very important date!" I dream of strangling that stupid hare. And doing it slowly, to make a point.

If I was launching a brand in an African market, I'd think hard about any lack of *Patience* in the customer experience. The valuegraphics for Africa would drive me to resolve that question, which is exactly what Valuegraphics Profiles are meant to do.

BALANCE

Africa is the only region on earth where *Balance* shows up in the top 10, so it's worth taking a bit of time to understand how it might impact your marketing.

According to Kasonde-van den Broek, *Balance* is a part of life and is always present. She told me how life in a developing part of the world can frequently mean you don't have what you need, so you learn to balance what you have. This plays out in the various roles people play in their personal lives, too. "Work, community, spirituality," she said. "You have to give time to all these parts of yourself or you are not complete."

She also shared a deeply personal experience: one of the traditional rituals that a man and a woman go through before marriage. "There are preparations and lessons that happen solely for the woman, and others for the man, but there is one ritual shared by both which is all about *Balance*. It's essentially an obstacle course made of mud and shells. The man and woman must navigate their way through together, in a way that teaches how important it is to maintain *Balance*."

Clearly, *Balance* is not something new that has emerged in response to contemporary conditions. It is a deep-rooted value, essential to understanding this part of the world.

My takeaway for marketers and creators is to look at *Balance* in a cautionary way. If the primary purpose of your brand is to help people succeed at some aspect of life, remember that a target audience who craves *Balance* might be put off by extremes. The popular Western stereotype of over-achieving, career-driven executives using your product to climb the corporate ladder at the expense of all else may not be relatable or desirable here. Equally off-putting could be a brand that is laser-focused on helping you optimize every minute of time for one reason or another.

It may seem like a big leap for me to say that these all-or-nothing approaches will not be as successful in Africa. But at least give me this: as *Balance* scores higher here than anywhere else on earth, it should make you stop and consider how to respond.

CHAPTER 13

THE VALUEGRAPHICS OF OCEANIA

ON AN EARLY MORNING BEACH WALK ONE DAY, YOU STOP and look at what's lying at your feet. It takes only a second or two for your brain to sort things into groups and help you make sense of the objects you can see. There are stones, shells, an assortment of driftwood, and a single feather.

You wonder about the welfare of the bird that lost that feather. You might question if the white piece of driftwood is from a different type of tree than the others, which are all dull gray. And you ponder the fate of a stone that reminds you of your mother-in-law. Should you put it in your pocket and take it home or throw it as far as you can into the sea?

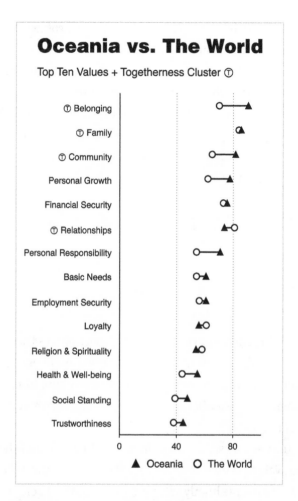

Oceania vs. The World

Top Ten Values + Togetherness Cluster ⓣ

ⓣ Belonging	
ⓣ Family	
ⓣ Community	
Personal Growth	
Financial Security	
ⓣ Relationships	
Personal Responsibility	
Basic Needs	
Employment Security	
Loyalty	
Religion & Spirituality	
Health & Well-being	
Social Standing	
Trustworthiness	

0   40   80

▲ Oceania   O The World

See what you did there? You instinctively clustered several objects into a few categories so that they made sense and you could think about them more easily. You could have also clustered things by size, by color, or by any other number of categories that seemed useful, depending on what you were trying to do.

The human brain can handle only seven things

simultaneously, so a typical Valuegraphics Profile of 10–15 values is outside our ability to process all at once. Clustering is a quick and easy way to understand what a collection of values is telling you about your target audience.

Let's have a look at the valuegraphics for Oceania[20] using clustering to help us make sense of what we see. Remember, these clusters are entirely of my own devising. Your own version could be as valid, if not more so.

THE STABILITY VALUES

- Financial Security

- Basic Needs

- Employment Security

Names for clusters are important to get right, as they can lead to wildly different outcomes. There are likely a half dozen other ways to give this cluster a working title, and choosing one should be influenced by the sector you are operating in.

If I were a recruitment firm, I could argue that these three values should be called the Survivalist Values. After all, these people highly value anything that will help them feel stable and unafraid of monetary turmoil. They want to know that they have money to live on and that there will be food on the table. On the other hand, a hotel group might want to call this cluster the Cost-Conscious Values because

---

20   Some context: Oceania is a geographic region that includes Australasia (Australia, New Zealand, and some neighboring islands), Melanesia, Micronesia, and Polynesia. Geographically speaking, it includes Hawaii, but we counted Hawaii as part of the United States because politically that's where it makes sense. Spanning the Eastern and Western Hemispheres, Oceania has a land area of 8,525,989 km² and a population of over 41 million. Source: "Oceania, April 19, 2022, https://en.wikipedia.org/wiki/Oceania

it would align better with the questions they are trying to answer. Using the same logic, a bank might want to name these the Fiscally Responsible Values.

From this point forward, I'm running with the Stability Values. I don't know why, but I am.

Let's pretend I'm the new SVP Marketing for LVMH in Oceania. The Stability Values would make me cautious about traditional luxury brand positioning. Emphasizing preciousness and extravagance might not fly here. But we could still make headway in this part of the world by stressing quality, craftsmanship, and care. It would be wise to remind our prospects that quality and craftsmanship lead to products that last a lifetime.

Leaving LVMH behind, let's think about a brand with intangible benefits. Spa services, for example, might seem like an unnecessary expense to the prototypical citizen of this region, unless you focus on the most tangible outcomes you can muster. Maybe you can deliver on stress reduction and clarity of mind. A refreshed perspective will help you perform better at work, after all, which impacts all the Stability Values. In other words, you'd want to make having a pedicure or a massage a necessity.

THE FORWARD-MOMENTUM VALUES

- Personal Growth

- Personal Responsibility

My shorthand definition of the value of *Personal Growth* is this: "being a better version of yourself each day." And I often describe people who highly value *Personal Responsibility* as "people who are happiest when they can get things done themselves." If you have a target audience who are driven to improve themselves and to get things done, they're probably focused on forward momentum.

Viewed through this lens, a gym membership is not about being fit; it's about creating a better version of yourself. A face cream is not about being beautiful; it's about choosing and using a product that reduces wrinkles. Buying a new home isn't about a place to live; it's about decisively moving along to the next stage of your life. You get the picture. These folks want to be moving forward, in the driver's seat, with both hands firmly on the steering wheel.

COMBINING CLUSTERS

We're already beginning to form a good mental picture of the people of Oceania. It's a sweeping mental picture of an entire region of the world with more than 40 million people, so it's about as oversimplified as you can get. Still, it's far better than what we could do with traditional demographic profiles.

Based on what we've pieced together so far, it seems OK to conclude that people from Oceania lean into life in a proactive way and are not big fans of risk. Now layer on the immense regional importance of *Community*, and we see these fine folks are interconnected and cautious contributors to progress. They want to see things move forward, and they are willing to shoulder their share of the responsibility for getting everyone to a good place in a good way. I like the sound of these people.

Let's connect the dots to marketing. For a change of pace, let's talk about not-for-profit organizations.

Any not-for-profit group in Oceania focused on arts, education, infrastructure, sports, environmentalism— aspects that make communities better—would have no trouble finding volunteers who wanted to shoulder some responsibility and lend a hand.

Let's say the staff at your company was keen to volunteer with Habitat for Humanity to build homes for people who need a leg up in life. Our valuegraphic insights for Oceania would suggest you could expand this idea beyond your own staff to include a broader *Community*. Why not encourage your followers, fans, prospects, and customers to join your team? That way, everyone can get to know each other while working together to achieve the same common goals.

And what if everyone who pitches in to help build those homes earns a free month of whatever your company provides, or a membership in a brand loyalty program, or some other financially beneficial incentive? That would leverage the Forward Momentum Values and the Stability Values in a *Community* project, a seemingly irresistible combination.

CHAPTER 14

THE VALUEGRAPHICS OF CENTRAL/ SOUTH AMERICA

SOMETIMES, LIKE ME, I BET YOU FIND YOURSELF IN SITUA-
tions where you are talking to people who already have a lot
on their mind. Asking them to think about complex things
like a Valuegraphics Profile for an entire region of the world
automatically makes their eyes glaze over.

And even though they might be nodding and smiling,
you know they are not hearing what you are saying. You
can tell they've started thinking about what they had for
lunch, if they remembered to rotate their tires this year,

if your shoes are as expensive as their shoes, or all sorts of other things.

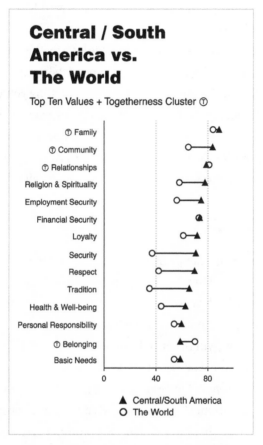

Central / South America vs. The World

Top Ten Values + Togetherness Cluster ⓣ

▲ Central/South America
O The World

Personification may be just what you need.

Personification, for our purposes, involves using your sociological imagination to imagine a single person who represents all the values contained in a Valuegraphics Profile.

This works because human brains love thinking about other humans. As soon as you convert data into a human, your brain happily hums along and enjoys itself. You can answer any marketing question that comes along by asking, "How would this person respond to this message?" or "What would influence this person to do what we'd like them to do?" And so on.

Plus, if you add some demographic information and some past-sales behavior from your customer database, you've got a ready-made "Customer Persona"—something you would normally pay a consultant a lot of money to dream up for you.

Let's use personification to help us understand the Valuegraphics Profile for Central/South America. I think we should give our new friend a name. We'll call him Luiz.

MEET LUIZ

Luiz is not in his happy place. In fact, he's in a terrible mood because he had to join a new gym (*Health & Fitness*).

He used to love working out at the gym down the street from his apartment, but he can't go there anymore. He had to join a new gym because he started a new job almost an hour away from where he lives. With the commute time and traffic being what it is, finding a new gym close to work was the only solution. He feels bad and sad to leave behind his friends from what he still calls his home gym. He feels like he's abandoned them (*Community, Relationships, Loyalty*). He knows it's silly to feel this way, but he can't help it.

Lifting weights helps Luiz stay fit and in top form for his responsibilities at work. But it's more than that. It's a kind of religious practice (*Religion & Spirituality*).

People who don't lift weights have a hard time understanding how the repetitive action of lifting something

Creating a Customer Persona Using the Three-Legged Stool

Let's talk about personas for a quick minute. Including valuegraphic source material for a persona will create a far more accurate working model of your prototypical customer than relying on demographics and psychographics alone. This essentially goes back to what we talked about in Part One and Chapter 3, about the three-legged stool of audience insights. Demographics and psychographics are all well and good, but without valuegraphics, all you know about your make-believe customer is who they are and what they've done so far. You don't know why they do the things they do.

Knowing that a 56-year-old white male bought an expensive electric fan made of brass is fine, but knowing that he places a lot of importance on Social Standing and Positive Environments points to why he bought that particular fan: he wants his home to look good while he's keeping comfy and cool.

Online shopping algorithms, which only have demographic and psychographic information to work with, will spend a month or two showing this fan purchaser advertisements and social content about buying fans, which makes no sense at all. He already bought one.

If that algorithm was as smart as you are, it would also consider the valuegraphics of that fan purchaser. This would lead to advertisements and social content about a beautifully designed composting bin or maybe some solid brass gardening tools with wooden handles and leather grips. Both of those products would further provide the Social Standing and Positive Environments he craves.

heavy and putting it back down again is akin to meditation, chanting, or rosary beads. You must concentrate to do it properly, which forces the mind to slow down and ignore all the busyness from the day. Luiz lifts weights to achieve clarity—to forget the emails, text messages, to-do lists, and other things that demand his attention from 9:00 a.m. to 5:00 p.m. every day of the week.

Joining a new gym doesn't sound like the end of the world to most people, but for Luiz, it meant a change in his social circle, and that's a big deal (*Community*). If he was writing a cover letter for a new job, he'd be forced to call himself a people person. He has a huge circle of friends and family, and it's easy to forget which are which (*Family, Relationships*). Being around other people and getting involved in their lives brings him a huge amount of joy. On the flip side, he feels edgy when he finds himself surrounded by new people. He doesn't feel like he belongs (*Belonging*).

Today, he is missing his home gym even more than usual because his new gym is busy. There are a lot of people working out, and counterintuitively, a busy weight room can be a solitary place. One of the unwritten rules of behavior in the weight room is to leave other people alone, and this social pressure to keep your distance means it can take a long time to get to know anyone (*Tradition*). But today, everyone around him seems to know everyone else, which means they've been regulars here for a long time. There's a lot of laughing and good-natured teasing, which only makes Luiz more aware of not fitting in.

The louder and more boisterous the people around him become, the more Luiz tries to block it out by focusing on the spiritual side of his weight-lifting practice. He thinks about each muscle involved in lifting each weight and the correct stance, movement, and form. Out of respect for everyone else and because it's another rule of weight-lifting etiquette, he meticulously wipes down each weight as he returns it to the correct position on the racks (*Respect*).

He wants to try to meet people and fit in here, but he knows that will only come with time. Besides, he's preoccupied with bigger issues right now (*Personal Responsibility*). His investment portfolio took a hit today (*Financial Security*). Each time his investment strategies don't work out, it compels him to learn more. He is anxious to get home and tackle another chapter of the investment book he is currently reading.

Every night after he gets home from the gym, Luiz reads books about being a smart investor (*Financial Security*). It's another part of his routine. He feels that lifting weights and investing his money are directly related. Both activities are about being resilient and responsible (*Security*). Plus, he knows that in order to provide for himself (*Basic Needs*) and be in control of his career (*Employment Security*), he must be physically and emotionally well—everything is related to everything else.

Moreover, he learns things from the gym that help him with his investments and vice versa. Both activities require persistent effort to yield slow, long-term gains. Both can have setbacks from calculated risks that misfire and require a quick change of plans to hasten recovery. In both cases, goals are best achieved through a careful combination of various tactics instead of a singular focus on only one path.

He saves each investment book on a special bookshelf in his bedroom (*Tradition*). He keeps them because they feel like trophies—souvenirs of his mental accomplishments. If somehow he misplaces one, he buys a new copy so the collection is always complete.

He knows that if his apartment was on fire in the middle of the night, on his way out the door, he'd grab his gym bag and quickly fill it with his framed photos of friends and family and his books because that's all he needs.

HOW TO USE PERSONIFICATION

Now that you've finished reading this, imagine Luiz represents your target audience. If you want Luiz to buy a car, download your app, or subscribe to your streaming video service, you know how to appeal to him because you have created a person who seems knowledgeable and even predictable.

Remember that this story was created as an example. After all, it's highly unlikely your target audience will ever be an entire region of the world! In Part Four, you will learn how to identify the values that matter to your specific target audience that you can use to craft a more precise personification. It's worth the time it takes to create one. It's a very handy tool that activates your sociological imagination.

CHAPTER 15

THE VALUEGRAPHICS OF THE MIDDLE EAST

I'LL NEVER FORGET WHAT HAPPENED AFTER THE FIRST speech I gave in the Middle East.

I was on a speaking tour of the region, and the first stop was the annual conference of the Middle East Council of Shopping Centers. It was a big crowd, with more than a thousand people from Bahrain, Saudi Arabia, and the United Arab Emirates. There are 18 countries in the Middle East, and most of them were represented.

Whenever I am asked to speak somewhere, I customize

my entire presentation by using a new Valuegraphics Profile that will help the people in the room. In this case, we found the shared values of people in the Middle East who go to shopping centers versus those who don't. It was my job to share the key findings with this crowd so they could engage their target audiences more effectively.

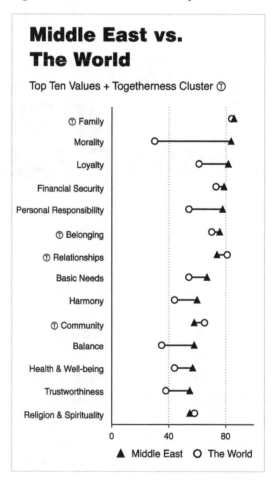

The morning of the speech, thanks to my foggy, jet-lagged brain, I'd grabbed the wrong attachment for my electric razor and accidentally shaved off half my beard. You can't undo that, so I had to shave the rest off, too. Consequently, I was beardless for the first time in close to a decade. It's a weird detail to share with you in a book, but it's evidence of my frame of mind.

As I walked beardless to the hotel ballroom to deliver my keynote, I could hear people around me speaking languages that were unfamiliar to my Western ears. Most people wore a national dress of one variety or another: men in long white tunics with traditional headgear and women in black, sometimes with only their eyes visible. It was quite impossible for me to feel like I was part of the crowd.

But what made me even more discombobulated was some of the findings from the Valuegraphics Profile for the region. One data point in particular. Nowhere else in the world does *Morality* show up in the number two spot, right after *Family*.

Morality shows up further down the rankings in other parts of the world, but it's not the headliner like it is in the Middle East. In the world of social science data, this is what is technically referred to as a very big deal, like discovering a new pyramid in Egypt or a lost civilization at the bottom of the ocean. And I was about to get on a stage and tell a room full of strangers that the second most important thing about them *was something entirely different from everywhere else in the world*. Ugh.

My speech went well despite everything. And as with all speaking gigs, as soon as I stepped off the stage, people started to drift over toward me for a follow-up chat.

One group of five women approached me. They were all

wearing traditional dress that left only their eyes exposed. One of them, who was holding a copy of my book, stepped forward and said, "It's important that you are here."

I wasn't sure what to make of that, so I kept quiet and waited for more.

"Demographics are an issue in this part of the world. Your message about changing the way we look at each other is something we talk about a lot."

Then the best thing happened. Another woman stepped forward and said, "And about *Morality*. Do not be worried about this finding. You are correct. We are taught as children to do the right things in the right way."

The women asked a few more questions and left. I walked back to my hotel room feeling quite pleased with myself. Valuegraphics had been well received; our message of demographic disruption had landed on a receptive audience, and the standout data on *Morality* had been confirmed.

There's a final part to this story about the importance of *Morality* in this region. My task after my speech that morning was to pack up, check out, and get on the road to the next gig in Abu Dhabi. I called room service and ordered a sandwich to eat while I folded my clothes and sorted through my papers.

The room service waiter who brought the sandwich was the same fellow who had brought me several meals in the last few days, and so I gave him a small box of one dozen Canadian maple sugar candies and thanked him for looking after me. He smiled from ear to ear, thanked me profusely, and left the room. The amazingly helpful team at the Canadian embassy had advised that I should bring some small token gifts from Canada with me, as they would be well received. And they were right.

Thirty minutes went by, and there was a knock at the door. I opened it, and there were seven members of the room service team. They had come to thank me, as they had all tried one of the maple sugar candies. They had signed a card for me and brought me some nuts and dried fruit for my trip.

This all seemed like an overreaction to a little box of candies, until the room service captain said, "It is rare that anyone thanks us. To repay your kindness is the right thing to do. We hope you have a safe journey and come back to visit us again soon, *inshallah*."

ETHNOGRAPHY IS THE MICRO TO OUR MACRO

Peter Bellini, who heads up PR and Influence for Memac Ogilvy in the UAE, introduced me to a dynamic duo who run an ethnographic research firm in the Middle East. Jamie Waskey and Milos Bugarcic started their firm, Wellspring, in 2017, and since then have been working for a roster of global clients and brands you'd recognize instantly if I was allowed to mention their names, which I'm not because for Jamie and Milos and all credible researchers, client confidentiality is crucial.

Wellspring does what ethnographic firms do best: collect consumer insights based on one-on-one interactions with individuals. There are numerous ways to do this, including focus groups and visiting people in their homes. The foundational underpinning of ethnographic work is that we can better understand how people behave by *watching* them behave rather than by asking them questions about how they behave.

In many ways, ethnographic work is the opposite of our methodology. Whereas Valuegraphics Profiles come from massive quantities of data about a target audience, ethnographers typically work with a small number of people and dive deep into the lives of each one. The valuegraphics and ethnography are like peanut butter and jam: delicious on their own but even better together.

Jamie, Milos, and I spent time looking at the valuegraphics for the Middle East versus the world. The resulting conversation was wide ranging, but of course the value of *Morality*, given its uniquely important role in the region, took center stage.

Jamie and Milos explained how hard it is to separate culture and *Morality* in the Middle East because they are inextricably intertwined. As an example, they talked about the practice of giving gifts to the poor during Ramadan.

The many ways that *Morality* shows up in daily life might also be why *Religion & Spirituality* is only on the top 10 list by a narrow margin and is no more important than it is for the rest of the world. The women who came to speak to me after I stepped off the stage in Dubai echoed this sentiment: the dominance of *Morality* was everywhere and existed *outside* of the influence of any specific religious beliefs and practices.

One of the most noticeable things when you are walking around in the Middle East is how covered up many people are. Many women are covered from head to toe in long black garments known by various names and designed to maintain various degrees of anonymity. But traditional dress for men is also extensive, with floor-length, long-sleeved robes and headgear that can cover almost all recognizable features. I'm treading lightly here and trying to be as respectful as I can. As an outsider, I know so little about this subject. I'm venturing out on this rather treacherous limb to reinforce one thing that Jamie and Milos said to me: that the modesty exhibited by these traditional forms of dress is rooted in *Morality*, too.

They told me a story about a taxi driver they met who explained that his wife didn't like going to the mall. Despite being covered from head to toe herself, she felt it was morally wrong to be there because she could still see everyone else. The taxi driver himself was shocked at this; he thought it was extreme.

Another observation from our ethnographic practitioners: there's a kind of "personal KPI" around *Morality*. Think about sitting down with one of your friends and how you would begin a conversation. In many cultures in the world, you would say something like, "How are you?" or "How's it going?" In the Middle East, a common response is something along the lines of "Morally, I'm doing well," or "I'm good with God," or "I'm working on my relationship with God." People judge themselves based on their overall *Morality* score.

Here's one more story from the Wellspring founders. I was showing Jamie and Milos some custom charts for various client target audiences so they could see what Valuegraphics Profiles look like at a more granular level.

One chart was for a target audience in the EU where the value of *Possessions* had scored highly, whereas in the regional data for the Middle East, this value didn't show up at all. The absence of that value reminded them of a story.

They had been hired by a global corporation to gather some specific information about a product category I can't mention, or you'd know exactly who the client was. This work they were doing involved in-home fieldwork—essentially, spending time with 18- to 24-year-olds who their client was keen to understand. One of the questions they asked of every research participant was "What is your most treasured possession?"

And here's the thing. No one understood the question. People said things like, "I guess I'd have to say my laptop?" Now imagine asking that question in the United States, where *Possessions* show up at roughly the midpoint on the top 10 list of most important values. What 18- to 24-year-old can you imagine in the United States who wouldn't have a laundry list of stuff that they felt attached to?

I included this story about *Possessions* for another reason. Sometimes the absence of data is data. The fact that *Possessions* did *not* make the cut for the top-10 list in the Middle East might be a key insight, depending on who is asking and what you are trying to do. If you are marketing possessions of some sort, it could, in fact, be the pivotal finding that dictates the direction of your entire strategy.

CHAPTER 16

THE VALUEGRAPHICS OF NORTH AMERICA (EXCEPT THE UNITED STATES)

I REMEMBER READING THOMAS MORE'S UTOPIA IN UNI-
versity. At least I remember *attempting* to read it.

It is a little book of political satire published in 1516.
It was written to poke fun at the ruling class of the day.
It describes a perfect society on a secret island. Only a

handful of travelers had ever managed to visit the place because, as the book explains, when the original discovery was announced, someone coughed while stating the exact location on the map. So the longitude and latitude were never accurately recorded.

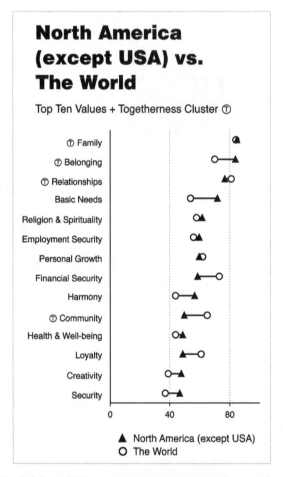

North America (except USA) vs. The World

Top Ten Values + Togetherness Cluster ⑦

▲ North America (except USA)
O The World

And although I'm not sure I ever managed to get through the dense text of the translated version (the original was in Latin), the idea of writing about a perfect but imaginary society has always stayed with me. It's a great way of pointing out problems and offering up solutions.

We can use the same technique to look at a Valuegraphics Profile and make it applicable to the marketing goals of an organization. Ask yourself, "What are the problems with the current situation, and what would be the perfect solution?" What is the perfect utopian solution your team can aspire to create for a product, service, or brand?

In this chapter, I'll create a utopian solution using the Valuegraphics for North America, except the United States.

But first, you may be wondering why we have excluded the United States. It was a judgment call.

North America is a collection of 23 countries. As a Canadian, part of me wanted to include a chapter on Canada. And I'm sure there will be readers from Mexico wondering why their great country hasn't been singled out for more focused analysis, too. But I had to make the cut somewhere, and the best way I can explain my reasoning is to point to Asia.

It would be irresponsible of me to write about Asia without recognizing the incredible influence on values that China has in that part of the world. So we created two regional profiles there: one for China and one for the rest of Asia. Separating the United States from the rest of North America follows the same line of thinking. If you want to read about the United States on its own, see Chapter 9.

One last thing before we dive headfirst into a mythical values-based utopian landscape: it's important to remember that this is not an exercise in actual product development. It's my attempt to help you understand a set of values from a Valuegraphics Profile and illustrate an idealized version of reality. Similarly, your team will likely never achieve the utopia that you create if you decide to use this powerful visualization tool. But remember that old famous saying by Norman Vincent Peale (who seemingly spent his life writing things that would become old famous sayings): "Shoot for the moon. If you miss, you'll land amongst the stars."

The values from the profile for North America (except the United States), which I've decided to focus on for the creation of this utopian product, are as follows:

- Relationships
- Employment Security
- Personal Growth
- Financial Security
- Harmony
- Health & Well-Being
- Loyalty

I chose these values because they appealed to me as most applicable to the make-believe organization where I am the imaginary director of marketing. They are the most applicable *and* they are a little bit of a stretch, which will make the task I have set for myself spicier.

Of course, if you are doing an exercise like this for your product, service, or brand, you could choose values based on other factors. You could decide, for example, to use only the top five most important values or only those values that score above the 50th percentile. You may even want to cherry-pick specific values because of some preexisting brand position that aligns with those values. It's up to you.

What follows is a utopian story about a perfect product for a fictitious corporation. As you read it, see if you can spot where the selected values make an appearance.

NORTHERN BANK

Chris was in the garden when the ring on his left hand vibrated. This happened only once or twice a year, so it always got his attention. He put down the trowel and the small specimen of wild Chinese ginger (*Asarum splendens*) that he was about to place in the hole he'd pried open in the earth. He went inside the cottage to see what was going on.

His ring was a gift from Northern Bank, which everyone refers to as NB. Chris had always thought the name was clever because the abbreviation NB also means *nota bene*, which is Latin for "note well" or "pay attention to this." And if there's one thing NB—the bank—is good at, it's paying close attention to things. That's why Chris pays a premium to belong to NB. They pay attention to every aspect of his financial life and more so he doesn't have to.

Today, however, the ring buzzing on his finger is a signal from Donna that something extraordinary needs his attention.

When you first become a member of NB, you have a series of meetings with a designated Life Banker. During those meetings, you establish threshold budgets for every aspect of your life and put a thousand little details in place so your mind is never cluttered with any of that ever again. Chris felt a kind of spiritual release when he handed over this responsibility to someone else. And Chris got lucky when he signed up. He was paired with Donna, the NB Life Banker everyone hopes they get.

Chris remembers their first meeting. Donna showed up right on time and sat in Chris's living room, although in reality, she was perched crisply on the edge of her sofa in her office thousands of miles away. Holographic meeting technologies are so seamless now that Chris was certain she was right there in the room with him, sipping tea and talking about his hopes, dreams, and frustrations.

This was the best part about belonging to NB as far as Chris was concerned. Those first meetings were a creative brainstorming session that was all about him. Donna was highly skilled in everything related to money, of course, but she was also a life coach, trained to help her clients look at their lives—and the possibilities that lay ahead—in a highly creative way.

NB took great pride in this particular way of doing business. Other banks had a fixed set of services and fee structures to match, but at NB, the services were customized and personalized to help each client achieve a life that they may not have ever thought possible.

Donna had helped Chris think about what might be and what could be and tell the difference between the two. She helped him create a picture of what the future would look like in a year, five years, ten years. She wasn't only there to make his dreams come true. She was there to show him better dreams.

After those initial meetings, Donna set the system up to look after everything. Every. Single. Thing. His bills were paid on time. His investments were managed. His checking account was never overdrawn. Rebates were applied for. Taxes were minimized and filed on schedule. Big expenses were incrementally saved for in advance of coming due, and he never had to think about any of it. Chris could focus on achieving the inner state of calm that he needed to be at his best, without any stress about anything financial. His money became an invisible and forgettable abstraction, which suited him perfectly.

When asked, Chris would explain his relationship with Donna this way: "Imagine if you had to think about all the details of your physical self. What if you had to remember to breathe on schedule, open and close heart valves, pump blood, and add the right chemicals to your digestive system at the right moments? Your brain would explode with stress. That's what my financial life was like before Donna. After Donna took over—*poof*! I've never had to think about it again."

Except very occasionally of course, like now. After every other possibility was explored, Donna would sometimes have no choice but to buzz his ring.

Chris sat on the sofa and pushed a flat button incised on his ring's surface three times. Donna materialized in his living room. She smiled and asked how the garden was coming along (her financial bedside manner was impeccable). She always made him feel safe and secure with an abundance of calm, attentive precision. This is why her clients loved her. They felt protected and cared for.

"Something's come up, Chris."

"I figured as much or you wouldn't be here," he replied with a grin.

"Yes, well, it's not an immediate problem, but it's serious enough that I needed to talk to you about it."

Chris leaned forward in his chair. "OK. Shoot. What's up?"

"Well, our monitoring systems show a change in your blood glucose levels. And not a temporary blip but an extended one." She tilted her head to one side and coyly looked at him with one eye. "Have you been eating too many sweets again?"

Chris felt his face flush. He knew it was for his own long-term health and well-being, but still, he didn't like being caught doing something he shouldn't.

"Chris, you know you have a family history of diabetes, and if this signal stays constant, I'll have to get the doctor involved. You know I care for you. You are my friend, and I want you to stay healthy for that reason alone. But it's also my job to make sure your life goals aren't smashed to pieces because of pastries and chocolates."

Chris felt ridiculous.

"I know. But I've been working longer hours than normal. And you know I work long hours most of the time anyway, so I'm working extra-long hours. And I sometimes feel like I deserve a treat. And that treat becomes expected, and then it's a habit, and well..."

He knew he wasn't making any headway, so he stopped mid-sentence and waited for her to say something.

"I understand. But let's put the brakes on. I'll keep a close eye on this. And if it gets better in, let's say, three weeks, we can forget all about this little chat." She smiled and stood up.

Chris was sullen, like a recalcitrant schoolboy. "OK. Thank you."

"You're welcome," Donna said brightly, trying to end on a positive note. "Bu, hey, listen. I've also brought good news with me. Your investments are doing well, and we can cash out on some sooner than we thought. So we've started interviewing contractors for your cottage renovations because I think we can get started now instead of next year."

"Really? Wow! That's amazing!" Chris was genuinely excited and forgot all the negative feelings from a few seconds ago. "Will there be enough for the outdoor sauna and plunge pool, too?"

"I think so. You might need to wait for those. But for sure, everything else can get done now. Isn't that great? This place is going to be spectacular."

"Thanks, Donna. I appreciate your help—with everything. You know that, I hope."

"I do. I know it. Now give me a hug."

After Donna disappeared and the holo-conference ended, Chris went back to the garden. He picked up the *Asarum splendens* and held it for a moment, looking at the roots and thinking about how big the leaves would become. He placed it into the hole he'd wedged in the earth and stood back to have a look at his morning's work. He liked what he saw.

USING THE UTOPIAN VISION

There are certain aspects of that utopian story that the make-believe bank where I am the make-believe director of marketing will never be able to achieve. But I should be pushing everyone to get as close as possible because the story is based on what our clients truly care about. The closer we get to achieving even a partial version of this utopia, the more we will engage our target audience. And the more engaging our target audience finds us, the better.

Here are some ideas about how this utopian vision could spark the right conversations and be more attainable than you might think.

For the hologram references to come true, the nascent hologram technologies available today will need to become far more advanced. But they do exist, and they are remarkable.[21] In the meantime, how can NB connect their advisors to their clients in a way that fosters the same meaningful relationships as described in the story? How close can you get to this ideal, given the technologies you can access today?

Is the communication ring Chris wears in this story possible? I already have a ring that tracks everything from my heart rate to my sleep cycles.[22] How long until this ring can track my finances and my blood glucose levels, too?

How can the bank shift to becoming a true partner in the *Financial Security* of their clients as well as their *Health & Well-Being* and *Harmony*? Given the amount of information we all share with digital entities like Google, why couldn't we foresee a time when banks are trusted enough to have this kind of robust data on clients, too?

---

21 It's often unwise to include developing technologies in a book because they will have progressed or disappeared by the time someone is reading this footnote. However, at the moment, one leader in the holoportation sector is online at portlhologram.com.

22 See OuraRing.com, with the same cautionary disclaimer as the previous footnote.

CHAPTER 17

THE VALUEGRAPHICS OF ASIA (EXCEPT CHINA)

I'VE WORKED WITH A LOT OF LARGE GLOBAL COMPANIES over the years in many sectors of the economy. Some were more product focused and others more customer focused.

In the product-focused corporations, sales and marketing are spoken of in one breath, like this: "sales'n'marketing." In those organizations, these two distinct roles are viewed as an amorphous blob of responsibilities that senior management has clumped together because they are the last step in the process after the product has been manufactured and is ready to ship.

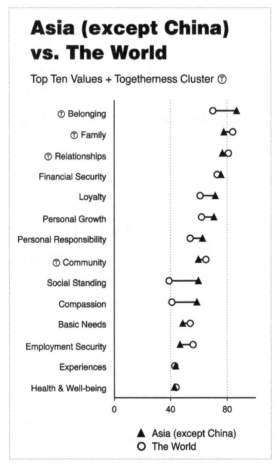

Asia (except China) vs. The World

Top Ten Values + Togetherness Cluster ⓣ

In the customer-focused organizations I've worked with, the reverse is most often true. Sales and marketing are separate kingdoms, with separate leadership, teams, budgets, and responsibilities.

Regardless of the kind of company structure you find

yourself in, I'm writing this book primarily for people who are interested in activating target audiences, so I expect most readers will have some responsibility for marketing objectives. However, in this chapter, I thought I'd take a look at valuegraphic data from a decidedly sales-oriented perspective.

Why? Because sales and marketing need each other. Marketing creates consumer interest for sales. What's the point of creating consumer interest without it leading to a transaction of some sort? And you can't sell things that no one is aware of. That's like standing in an empty room with the blinds down and the door closed and wondering why no one knows you are there. Like it or not, sales and marketing will be holding hands forever.

In case you are wondering, this chapter on the values of the people of Asia excludes China because, well, China is so enormously influential in this part of the world—and everywhere in fact—that I've given that country a chapter to itself. You can read about the valuegraphic data for China in Chapter 11.

I started work on this chapter by posting a few pleas for help on LinkedIn and other social channels. I wanted to talk to senior sales leaders about the valuegraphics for this part of the world. One of the things I love about LinkedIn is how willing people are to pitch in. And sure enough, a wonderfully helpful fellow named Anshul Punetha reached out and offered to introduce me to some of his contacts. I'm grateful for his assistance. Because of his kindness, I ended up having the most fascinating conversations.

When we spoke, Rakesh Kumar had wrapped up a role

as managing director and South Asian GM for SC Johnson (Ziploc! Brillo! Glade!). His previous posts included stints at PepsiCo (Lay's! Gatorade! Pepsi and 7 Up!) and Conagra Foods (Duncan Hines! Reddi -Wip! Orville Redenbacher's!).

I also spoke with Anup Mangaserri, currently VP of consumer products for India with the Goodyear Tire Company, with prior experience as SVP at CEAT, another tire-producing megacorp. His background includes executive roles where he was responsible for other consumer products like candy (Perfetti van Melle) and paint (ICI Paints).

What follows is a combined set of observations culled from extensive conversations with these two sales leaders. Both men were so generous with their time, and I can't thank them enough for their help.

VALUEGRAPHICS DATA FROM A SALES PERSPECTIVE

People in this part of the world are notoriously friendly and willing to strike up a conversation with whomever they happen to be standing next to. This gregariousness likely stems from the enormous importance of *Belonging*. It's as if everyone is at a big, crowded kitchen party, 24/7/365. You can't be in the middle of a kitchen party without saying something to the people next to you.

For brands operating in this part of the world, the importance of *Belonging* can be a powerful tool. For example, both Anup and Rakeesh gave me examples of how single-use packaging helped people get the *Belonging* they desired and revolutionized certain product categories, too. The urge to buy the same brand as everyone else is strong, but since the vast majority of the population in India makes precious little money, the only way to act on this urge is to buy enough shampoo, candy, or whatever for one day.

Rakeesh told me about seeing this play out in small villages, where a mom would do without things in her own life to make sure her child had Frito Lay's potato chips because even though she might not be able to afford the best of everything, she could at least make sure her child had the most well-known bag of chips (or "crisps" as they are called in many parts of the world). *Social Standing* starts to figure into this conversation, too, as well-known brands serve as a way to signal prosperity, however relative that prosperity may be.

My marketing brain leaps into action here, and I wonder if *Belonging* could be harnessed in other ways. Membership-based brands would likely thrive. And even in a B2B setting, anything that could make clients feel like insiders would be a safe bet. When I asked about this, Anup confirmed my hunch. He told me about the enormous success he'd seen with annual award programs and certifications for channel partners and retailers.

Award programs would likely activate so many of the most magnetic values here: *Loyalty*, *Social Standing*, *Personal Growth*, *Belonging*, *Relationships*...anyone working in this part of the world would do well to ask themselves if they are doing enough to recognize, reward, and elevate their partners in every way they can.

From my conversations, I learned that many parents in India push their children toward *Belonging*, as it is seen as a necessary condition for success. Some of the most desirable jobs are with multinational corporations and governments because they provide *Financial Security*. But in order to get these jobs, it's vital to not stand out from the crowd or call undue attention to yourself. Anup referenced how Western cultures often glorify individualism and how Westerners often self-confidently assume that they will be accepted for who they are. He used a phrase that several of my Asian friends have used many times but that I've never had context for until now. He said children are taught to subsume individuality and "go with the flow."

I can think of a dozen brands that are about exactly the opposite. Brands that have successfully carved out a niche by helping consumers be individuals and break away from the crowd. I have a sneaky suspicion that these brands would need to rethink things in any culture where there is a clear preference for fitting in.

Would MAC cosmetics be successful by encouraging consumers to "celebrate your style, heart and soul" and using spokespeople like RuPaul? Would Jones Soda have had as much of a runaway hit in India by letting everyone send in photos for their own pop labels instead of sporting the same photos as all the other bottles on the shelf? I don't know how popular Apple computers are compared to the alternatives in India and elsewhere in Asia, but I wonder if the much-discussed Think Different campaign that celebrated famous nonconforming outliers worked as well in Asia as it did in other regions of the world. I'd love to ask a certain fast-food giant if their customers in Asia want to "Have It Your Way" or if they prefer to "Have It the Most Popular Way."

We also talked about the value of *Compassion*. Rakeesh explained that *Compassion* acts as a kind of social safety net. You need to be kind to those around you because you never know when you will be the one who needs a helping hand. I brought up what you might call "compassionate brands" like Toms shoes, which donates a pair of shoes to someone in need for every pair they sell. Anup didn't think this would work as well in India because it's desirable for displays of *Compassion* to be far more localized. It's better to help the people from your village, your town, or your region than it is to help "someone who needs shoes somewhere" in another part of the world, he explained. "People like to see their compassion at work right before their eyes."

A thought popped into my head about this point. I wonder if micro-philanthropy would be a popular structure here. Micro-philanthropy is a term used to describe small donations from many people. It might be a powerful thing for brands to give consumers the ability to choose where corporate donations are made. In a world where we can connect a billion people to a billion things through platforms like eBay and Amazon, surely there is a way I can purchase a pair of sneakers and donate a buck to whatever cause I feel connected to. That could be fiercely powerful in India, in Asia, and I suspect in many other parts of the world, too.

CHAPTER 18

A GLANCE IN THE REARVIEW MIRROR

I HOPE YOU'VE ENJOYED YOUR VALUEGRAPHIC WORLD tour and had some fun using your sociological imagination while you were at it. Travel is always such a mind-expanding pursuit, don't you think? And please don't worry if your ability to summon up and deploy your sociological imagination isn't second nature as yet—it will take a bit of practice. If you keep working at it, you'll soon be looking at everything around you through this new inquisitive lens.

Here's an important distinction to remember: nothing we've done is arbitrary. We're not lumping a whole bunch of people together and assuming they like this or that. It's a stereotype to assume millennials like avocado toast, men are emotionally bereft, or baby boomers are bad with technology. But when our data shows that people in China place a great deal of importance on *Family*, that's a statistical fact.

Here's a recap of the tools and techniques we used in the previous chapters.

PATTERN MAKING (Chapter 8)

Looking at the data and making patterns out of what you see is a crucial step toward interpreting valuegraphic data and Valuegraphics Profiles in a way that can be useful for your organization.

Also remember that the *absence* of a pattern or the absence of data can be valuable as well. For example, *Financial Security* does not show up as one of the three most important values in the United States. The absence of this value tells you something about the American people.

COMPARISONS (Chapter 9)

Sometimes it is easier to understand a thing if you compare it to another thing. Apples are red and sweet and juicy. All true. But if you sit an apple beside a banana, you suddenly realize that apples are also round and do not require peeling.

CONTEXTUAL READING (Chapter 12)

A crucial part of analyzing valuegraphic data is understanding the context in which that data exists. It will help you interpret those values correctly and see their vast implications. If you're unfamiliar with your audience or with the market you're launching in, always look for what others have written about the subject.

CLUSTERING (Chapter 13)

Because the human brain can process only about seven things at once, a list of too many values can be overwhelming. Try clustering them into groups that make sense to you and give those groups a name that both reflects the values and addresses what you want to achieve with the data. These customized clusters will help everyone involved make sense of the values and how to use them.

PERSONIFICATION (Chapter 14)

Creating client personas is an age-old marketing practice, and including valuegraphic data will make your personas better. Think of the three-legged stool of audience insights and weave your valuegraphics into and around whatever demographic and psychographic details you have. It'll give you a clear idea of your target audience and how they will behave.

ETHNOGRAPHIC QUESTIONING (Chapter 15)

Ethnography is based on watching how people behave. Short of hiring ethnographic researchers to help you, there are ways of thinking you can borrow from this practice. If you are fortunate enough to have both valuegraphic and ethnographic insights for your target audience, that's really the best case of all.

UTOPIAS (Chapter 16)

Often, speculating about a perfect world is a powerful way to get your sociological imagination working. Look at the valuegraphics for your target audience, and then dream up an ideal scenario inspired by core human values. If you are doing this right (and thinking big!), you'll have included ideas that are not achievable, at least for now. This is fine because the point is to have a goal to move toward, a North Star of sorts.

IT'S TIME TO DIY

Now that you know a bit more about the values of people around the world and have practiced using your sociological imagination, how do you apply these learnings to your company? In the next part of this book, I'll talk you through how we do it—how my company creates custom Valuegraphics Profiles for the organizations we work with. Then I'll give you a DIY toolkit and explain a simple process so you can get started on your own.

PART FOUR

THE DIY VALUEGRAPHICS TOOLKIT

CHAPTER 19

HOW WE CREATE CUSTOM PROFILES

EVERY ORGANIZATION WANTS TO INFLUENCE THE DECI-
sions that people make. And since our values drive all our
decisions, it stands to reason that organizations must identify the values of the people they want to reach.

The trick is, of course, to identify which values your
entire target audience *shares in common* so you can appeal
to them as a group. In short, you need their valuegraphics. Here's how my company goes about creating a custom
Valuegraphics Profile for the companies and organizations

that hire us. This is good for you to know because it will help you see the logic behind the DIY version that follows.

THE THEORY

Let's start with the basics. We know that each of us is driven to chase some number of the 56 possible core human values in some order of importance. This unique combination of values is the operating system for our life; it determines everything we do.

So in order to engage a target audience, we need to know what values the members of that target audience share. That tells us how to create products, services, brands, or ideas that will influence the whole group.

With me so far? Let's dive a little deeper.[23]

FINDING THE RIGHT VALUES IN THE DATABASE

The first thing we do, alongside whoever else is involved, is write a precise description of the target audience we want to understand. You can think of this as putting a metaphorical fence around a group of people so we know who is inside the group and who isn't.

Next, we find people who match the target audience description—enough people to make our sample statistically accurate.

Then we ask them a few questions.

Let's say a dental products company is interested in

---

23 For more granular information about our methodologies, please visit valuegraphics.com.

knowing the shared values of men living in Beijing who have a college degree and use a lot of dental floss. Let's call them the Flossaholics. These guys floss at least twice a day, seven days a week. They love flossing.

Next up, we find a group of these floss fanatics in Beijing large enough to be statistically accurate, and we ask them a few questions. We ask them to tell us about themselves, the kind of floss they like best, how much floss they use with each pull from the package, and so on. Then we get to the good stuff: we ask them to tell us what they value most of all. Not what they value about dental floss specifically, but what their values are for their life. Then we probe deeper about each of those values.

People tell us the most remarkable things. The patterns and signals we see give us the secret code we need to unlock our 750,000-survey benchmark database and identify the right data to pull out. Put simply, we profile a sample audience and extrapolate rich data profiles from the Valuegraphics Database.

Thanks to that methodology, we end up with a Valuegraphics Profile.

Once you know the valuegraphics of your target audience, there is still a lot of work to be done. Deciding how to execute on that newfound information, the strategies and tactics you devise to achieve your objectives, how you connect the dots between what you've got and what people want—all of that is up to you. *Valuegraphics will simply point you to the right questions.* As a final step, we teach our clients how to answer those questions using their expertise, their experience, and their sociological imagination.

PLAYING THE PIANO
WITH YOUR FISTS

The methodology I've described above is how we work one-on-one with individual organizations that want the most granular and precise profiles possible. But custom profiles are not for everyone.

That's why we created a do-it-yourself (DIY) version for this book. In the next chapter, I'll explain how to use the DIY version, which is a bit like playing the piano with your fists. It's not the same as a concert pianist playing a grand piano on the stage of the Sydney Opera House, but you will be able to bang out some music, and you will be using the *right* instrument! It is a far, far better thing to be bashing away on the valuegraphic piano than it is to keep using the broken, discarded, demographic guitar that someone has—quite rightfully—tossed in a dark corner backstage.

Ready to learn how to do this yourself?

CHAPTER 20

DIY VALUEGRAPHICS: A FOUR-STEP GUIDE

I WISH THERE WAS A PHYSICAL BOX OF COMPONENT PARTS that you could actually hold right now, like a box containing a Björksnäs from IKEA. Because if there was, you could metaphorically lay the particleboard panels, dowel tips, and hexagonal screws on the floor, follow the instructions, and slowly but surely assemble a bedside table.

But alas, it's not so simple. The component parts of a Valuegraphics Profile can be used to create many things, and your own experience and intuition are essential parts of this project. As a result, the step-by-step guide is fairly open-ended. In other words, you could make a bedside table or a dining room china hutch with the same kit of parts.

Your understanding of the initiatives your organization has tried before is vital. Your knowledge of the competitive landscape and what everyone else in the sector is trying to do with their target audience is indispensable. That sneaky suspicion you've had for a long time about what could be a winning strategy might come into play. All of these factors inform the outcome—what your sociological imagination will make of it.

This is why our research methodologies were designed to provide you with the *right questions* and why we leave the answers up to you. We can show you the North Star you should be following, but you will need to chart your own course. But it's worth it because if you connect what you have to offer to what your customers value, you will have customers for life.

Below is a quick overview of the DIY process, an executive summary. Don't worry if it feels a bit confusing at first. I will deep dive into each step in the chapters that follow, and I will explain the resources you need to make the step a success. For now, here's the plan as a whole so that you know how it all works together.

STEP ONE:
Send Out the Quiz and Tally the Results

The first thing you need to do is find a way to reach your target audience and send them the Valuegraphics Archetype Quiz. It's called an archetype quiz because there are 15 archetypes in the global database. Think of them as 15 tribes. Everyone on earth (near enough everyone, at least) fits into an archetype.

You could send out the quiz using the customer contact information you have in your database. You could reach out to potential prospects through a trade association. You could even go back to basics and shove a printed copy of the quiz into all your shopping bags or product packaging and offer a small incentive—a chance to win a gift certificate, for example—if people fill it out.

Be creative and find as many ways as you can to get the quiz out into the world. The more people from your target audience who respond, the more accurate the results will be. And people will not mind being asked. Generally speaking, people are happy to answer questions they find intriguing and related to things they care about, which this quiz most definitely is.

And as tempting as it is to take the quiz yourself, it was never intended to work for individuals. It was designed to poll large groups and determine which archetype is most representative of the *entire* group. There's no harm in taking the quiz yourself of course, but it just won't be as accurate for one person as it will be for many.

Once you've collected all the responses, it's time to tally them up. Chapter 21 includes the quiz questions as well as the answer key.

STEP TWO:
Find Your Superhero, Sidekick, and Nemesis Archetypes

The quiz results will point you to the Valuegraphics Archetype that most closely resembles your target audience.

This is your primary archetype, or what we call your Superhero Archetype.

Part Five of this book includes a chapter for each of the 15 different archetypes, so you can flip over there and look up their valuegraphics, plus other useful data and insights.

It might also be a prudent idea to take a look at two other archetypes other than your Superhero Archetype.

If a second archetype scores quite high—if there's only a few points that separate the Superhero Archetype from the one that comes next—you've got yourself a Sidekick Archetype. This isn't a good thing or a bad thing; it's simply a fact. Many of the best superheroes out there have sidekicks, after all. Where would Batman be without Robin, or Superman without Lois Lane?

Have a look at the chapter for your Sidekick Archetype, and compare the information against the Superhero Archetype. Pay particular attention to any values that both groups have in common because those will be extra powerful, the most valuable values of all.

And finally, it can be intriguing to look at the *lowest*-scoring archetype for your quiz respondents—your Nemesis Archetype. If you understand what the people in your target audience value *the least*, it adds another layer of insight to what you know.

STEP THREE:
Check the Charts for Your Region

Now compare the valuegraphics for your archetype with the values for the region you are working in, which you will find back in Part Three of this book. Watch for similarities or differences that might be worth thinking about further.

Here's an example. Let's say you are in the business of designing, making, and selling expensive wristwatches. And let's assume you've discovered that your Superhero Archetype highly values *Personal Growth.*

On its own, that's a useful thing to know. Anything you can do to connect the dots between your product and how it will help your customers achieve more *Personal Growth* will make your timepieces absolutely irresistible. How can your wristwatch help someone become a better version of themselves? How can it help them be smarter about how they use their time, or perhaps more present in every moment, or even more aware of how precious time is? Can you build those benefits into your product as features so the value of *Personal Growth* manifests itself in a physical way? How can your positioning and messaging crank the volume on those ideas to levels that become impossible to ignore?

Now let's say you sell your watches in Europe, so you go back to the regional chapters and have a look at the values for the EU.

There, you discover that *Personal Growth* is the sixth most important value in all of Europe. You also see what values are more important than *Personal Growth* (for example, *Experiences* rank higher) and which ones, like *Possessions*, are less important. You might learn from this chart that the watch itself (*Possessions*) is less important than the act of *getting* the watch (*Experiences*). That would lead to a set of strategic decisions that you might otherwise not make.

And if you are thinking about expanding your retail operations into another market, you might want to see how *Personal Growth* figures in the lives of people in other parts of the world. It would help you decide where to establish your first non-European outpost.

That was a brutal sledgehammer of an example. In a real-world situation, the questions and conversations would be far more complex and nuanced because someone who knows something about manufacturing wristwatches would be using their sociological imagination, instead of me. But the theory still holds: checking the values of your archetype against the values of your region yields great insights.

The fact is, there's no real hard-and-fast set of rules to follow, given how generalized and enormous the archetype and regional datasets are. You are looking for hints. You are hunting for clues. You are scanning for patterns. You want to find anything that seems to be encouraging or that might be a red flag. That's why we spent Part Three expanding your sociological imagination so you are prepared to think about valuegraphic data in a more meaningful way.

STEP FOUR:
The Values Thinking Process

Now it's time to bring all the data together to create actionable insights. We call this process Values Thinking.

Values Thinking is nothing more than a focused brainstorming method. It helps you generate actionable ideas while keeping the shared values of your target audience at the center of everything you do.

We'll break down the Values Thinking process in Chapter 23. For now, in the next chapter, let's begin with Step One: The Valuegraphics Archetype Quiz.

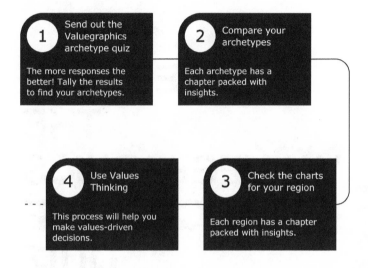

1 Send out the Valuegraphics archetype quiz

The more responses the better! Tally the results to find your archetypes.

2 Compare your archetypes

Each archetype has a chapter packed with insights.

4 Use Values Thinking

This process will help you make values-driven decisions.

3 Check the charts for your region

Each region has a chapter packed with insights.

CHAPTER 21

STEP ONE: THE VALUEGRAPHICS ARCHETYPE QUIZ

THE DIY VALUEGRAPHICS ARCHETYPE QUIZ IS A SET OF 15 questions you can use with any target audience to determine which Valuegraphics Archetype they resemble most.

This simple quiz is a rough-and-ready way to access the 15 most powerful tribes or cohorts inside the Valuegraphics Database. Most of the population of the world fits into at least one of these archetypes almost all of the time, so your target audience will, too.

As I've said before, it's like playing the piano with your fists. It's not a precise and elegant piece of music you are making here, but at least you are using the enormous power of shared human values to better understand the people you want to reach. Even banging out a rough tune will be better than continuing to use old-fashioned demographic stereotypes!

Use your favorite online survey tool and collect as many responses from your target audience as you can. Tabulation instructions follow the questions below.

THE QUIZ

For each of the statements that follow, please circle a number from one to ten that represents how you see yourself in relation to that statement. There are no right or wrong answers. Your first reaction is correct! Take your time and please choose only one number for each question.

I don't feel entirely settled in my life, for many reasons.

Not like me at all — 0 1 2 3 4 5 6 7 8 9 10 — Very much like me

I feel better when I'm on top of the family finances. Someone has to make sure the bills get paid.

Not like me at all — 0 1 2 3 4 5 6 7 8 9 10 — Very much like me

I am most content when I have time to be creative. It's one of the most important things in my life.

Not like me at all — 0 1 2 3 4 5 6 7 8 9 10 — Very much like me

I've found that people, places, and things help me be the best version of myself. Change for the sake of change is risky; you never know how it will turn out.

Not like me at all — 0 1 2 3 4 5 6 7 8 9 10 — Very much like me

I work a lot, but I don't mind because it means I can live the life that motivates me the most.

Not like me at all — 0 1 2 3 4 5 6 7 8 9 10 — Very much like me

As long as I have a secure job with a steady income, I can spend more time focused on what matters: my family and my friends.

Not like me at all — 0 1 2 3 4 5 6 7 8 9 10 — Very much like me

I want everything and everyone important in my life to be kind, gracious, and balanced.

Not like me at all — 0 1 2 3 4 5 6 7 8 9 10 — Very much like me

The environment is the issue of our time, and each of us must do our part. I wish I knew how to help more.

Not like me at all — 0 1 2 3 4 5 6 7 8 9 10 — Very much like me

The best way to keep growing as a person is to get out there and do things and interact with the world.

Not like me at all — 0 1 2 3 4 5 6 7 8 9 10 — Very much like me

I am not into having stuff, owning stuff, or collecting stuff. Stuff weighs me down.

Not like me at all — 0 1 2 3 4 5 6 7 8 9 10 — Very much like me

My family and I live a considered life. We plan for the future and work toward our goals in a routine way.

Not like me at all — 0 1 2 3 4 5 6 7 8 9 10 — Very much like me

Live a good life, be kind to others, and honor your family—these are the keys to happiness.

Not like me at all — 0 1 2 3 4 5 6 7 8 9 10 — Very much like me

Technology keeps me connected to the things I care about and in touch with the people I love.

Not like me at all — 0 1 2 3 4 5 6 7 8 9 10 — Very much like me

It is important to devote some time each day to my religious/spiritual self.

Not like me at all — 0 1 2 3 4 5 6 7 8 9 10 — Very much like me

If living my best life and being the best version of me means using my credit cards to pay for experiences, that's fine with me. What else are they for?

Not like me at all — 0 1 2 3 4 5 6 7 8 9 10 — Very much like me

HOW TO TABULATE THE RESULTS

For each question, add up the responses. Here's an example.

Let's say you had 100 people answer the quiz.

If 50 of your respondents answered the first question by choosing number 5 on the scale of 0–10, and the other 50 chose number 2, you'd calculate the score for that question like this:

50 people chose number 5: 50 × 5 = 250

50 people chose number 2: 50 × 2 = 100

Question Score   350

Now do the same thing, and come up with a score for each question.

WHAT DO THE SCORES MEAN?

Each question on the survey relates to a different Valuegraphics Archetype. The first question corresponds to the first archetype on the following list. The second question corresponds to the second archetype, and so on.The question that receives the highest score indicates the archetype that is most important for your target audience—your Superhero Archetype. If a second question scores fairly close, that's your Sidekick Archetype. And the question that scores the lowest is your Nemesis Archetype, which can be a great source of insight, too.

In the next chapter, let's take a broad look at the valuegraphic data you'll be examining in Steps Two and Three.

	Quiz Question	Your Score	Archetype	Chapter Number
1	I don't feel entirely settled in my life, for many reasons.		Seekers	25
2	I feel better when I'm on top of the family finances. Someone has to make sure the bills get paid.		Frugal	26
3	I am most content when I have time to be creative. It's one of the most important things in my life.		Creatives	27
4	I've found that people, places, and things help me be the best version of myself. Change for the sake of change is risky; you never know how it will turn out.		Loyalists	28
5	I work a lot, but I don't mind because it means I can live the life that motivates me the most.		Workers	29
6	As long as I have a secure job with a steady income, I can spend more time focused on what matters: my family and my friends.		Savers	30
7	I want everything and everyone important in my life to be kind, gracious, and balanced.		Harmonious	31
8	The environment is the issue of our time, and each of us must do our part. I wish I knew how to help more.		Environmentalists	32
9	The best way to keep growing as a person is to get out there and do things and interact with the world.		Adventurers	33
10	I am not into having stuff, owning stuff, or collecting stuff. Stuff weighs me down.		Anti-materialists	34
11	My family and I live a considered life. We plan for the future and work toward our goals in a routine way.		Steady	35
12	Live a good life, be kind to others, and honor your family—these are the keys to happiness.		Moral	36
13	Technology keeps me connected to the things I care about and in touch with the people I love.		Connectors	37
14	It is important to devote time each day to my religious/spiritual self.		Spiritual	38
15	If living my best life and being the best version of me means using my credit cards to pay for experiences, that's fine with me. What else are they for?		Spenders	39

CHAPTER 22

STEPS TWO AND THREE: VALUEGRAPHICS ARCHETYPES AND REGIONAL PROFILES

YOU ARE SITTING IN A BUBBLE BATH

SHARP READERS OF MY LAST BOOK, *WE ARE ALL THE*
Same Age *Now*, will recognize the bubble bath analogy

that follows. Truth is, I've yet to find a better way to describe how the Valuegraphics Archetypes work.

The Valuegraphics Database is an enormous and complex sociological dataset. It contains the responses to 750,000 surveys about 436 metrics in 152 languages and covers nine regions of the world that encompass 180 countries. Trying to describe all that data, what it means, and how it coalesces into archetypes that can be used to describe vast swaths of the global population is a daunting task unless you have an advanced degree in sociology, a ton of experience in statistics, and you know the intricacies of SPSS files like the back of your hand. You'd also need to understand continuous dimensions, cultural cognition, and something called fuzzy data.

It's a heck of a lot easier to talk about a bubble bath.

Imagine yourself sitting in a big, frothy bubble bath like a benevolent ancient god looking out over the bubble-based world in front of you. As your gaze moves across the bubble landscape, you see patterns and shapes. Some unseen force causes the bubbles to clump together into mountain peaks in some areas and disperse to form valleys in others.

There are short mountains and tall mountains. Some have a broad base, and others are more like spires. The valleys come in all shapes and sizes, too. The more you look, the more you see infinite types of mountains, hills, valleys, and plains, all made up of bubbles.

Every bubble in the bathtub is a data point. The data clumps together and forms peaks in some places and disperses into valleys in others.

When we scan the global dataset, we can see 15 dominant

spires of data, what you might call the Himalayas of the bubble bath landscape. Each of these 15 data peaks has been named after a powerful force—a unique variable—that causes the data to clump together.

These 15 unique variables attract data points like a magnet. The stronger the variable, the more data is drawn toward it and the bigger the spire of data becomes. We call these 15 biggest, most influential data spires the Valuegraphics Archetypes.

People who identify with one of these 15 variables agree with everyone else who identifies with that variable about most things in life, pretty much all the time.

Stop here for a moment and read that last sentence again. This is perhaps the most important finding from all the work we've done.

Not only are there 15 spires of data formed around these unique variables, but all the people in each group *agree on pretty much everything, pretty much all the time.* They agree as much as 89% of the time, in fact. These are tribes. Tribes of like-minded people who are extremely similar to each other, drawn together because of one powerfully magnetic and unique variable that they share. Now compare that to the complete lack of similarity that exists among members of any demographic tribe, who agree, on average, roughly 10.5% of the time. Demographics tell us hardly anything about who people really are.

The 15 archetypes are:

1.   The Seekers

2.   The Frugal

3. The Creatives

4. The Loyalists

5. The Workers

6. The Savers

7. The Harmonious

8. The Environmentalists

9. The Adventurers

10. The Anti-materialists

11. The Steady

12. The Moral

13. The Connectors

14. The Spiritual

15. The Overspent

STEPS TWO AND THREE: THE PRACTICALITIES

These two steps are relatively straightforward, but let's recap anyway. Based on the results of your Valuegraphics Archetype Quiz (Step One), you should have identified the Superhero Archetype for your target audience.

Step Two is the moment where you learn more about your Superhero Archetype—and what they value—by looking them up in the archetypes section, which begins with Chapter 25. If you have a Sidekick Archetype, you can look that up, too.

For Step Three, look at the regional charts, which

begin with Chapter 8. Cross-checking the valuegraphics of your Superhero Archetype with the relevant regional profiles gives you two valuable datasets to compare and draw insight from.

A MURKY GRAY DISCLAIMER

I live in a world of murky gray. Since beginning work on the Valuegraphics Database back in 2011, learning to love the murky gray has been one of the most difficult things I've had to do. Like most people, I often wish there was a simple black or white response to everything. But is there ever? Maybe things are clear and finite if you study mathematical theorems, where one plus one will always equal two. But that's an extremely rarefied world to inhabit.

Most of the time, when we reach a fork in the road, we are faced with decisions between the lesser of two evils or the greater of two goods. In fact, there are countless clichés about making a call, choosing a horse, placing a bet, going with your gut, following your nose...a clear indication that we all live in the same murky gray world.

Using the archetype reference chapters and the regional profile chapters is the same as anything else in life. You do your best, collect as much information as you can, have a good think about it, and then make a decision. If you were hoping for a definitive binary answer to whatever questions you have about your target audience, I'm sorry. It's not going to happen here or anywhere else for that matter. All you can do is analyze the most accurate insights you can get your hands on and make the most well-informed decision you can.

However, you are about to take a great leap forward. There will be an enormous improvement in the accuracy of your decisions if you follow the steps in this book. Soon you will be able to engage and activate your target audience more powerfully because you will know the values that drive the decisions they make.

Here's an example. Let's assume you have sent the Valuegraphics Archetype Quiz to your target audience and discovered that your Superhero Archetype is the Seekers (Chapter 25).

Globally speaking, you've won the archetype lottery, my friend, because the Seekers are the most aligned and most dominant archetype on Planet Earth. A full 21% of the world's population fit into this archetype, and they are valuegraphically aligned 85% of the time. If this is the archetype that is the best match for your target audience, they will be quite easy to activate if you connect the dots between your brand and what they care about—what they value most of all.

Now let's compare those numbers to a demographically defined target audience. Millennials, for example, agree with each other only 16% of the time. That means, if you make a decision based on what you know about the Seekers, you have an 85% chance of doing something that will generate a response, compared to a 16% chance if you use what you know about millennials. Millennials are not similar enough to activate a satisfying response, regardless of what you say or do.

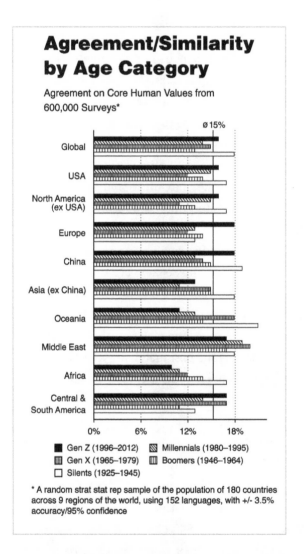

Agreement/Similarity by Age Category

Agreement on Core Human Values from 600,000 Surveys*

Ø 15%

- Global
- USA
- North America (ex USA)
- Europe
- China
- Asia (ex China)
- Oceania
- Middle East
- Africa
- Central & South America

0%   6%   12%   18%

- ■ Gen Z (1996–2012)
- ▩ Millennials (1980–1995)
- ▦ Gen X (1965–1979)
- ▥ Boomers (1946–1964)
- ☐ Silents (1925–1945)

* A random strat stat rep sample of the population of 180 countries across 9 regions of the world, using 152 languages, with +/- 3.5% accuracy/95% confidence

So congratulations! If the work you've done so far points to a target audience of Seekers (85%) instead of millennials (16%), your chances of making something good happen are more than five times better, simply by changing the way you look at your target audience. Nifty stuff.

But this seemingly clear-cut and celebratory step

forward could be an enormous downer, too, because it depends on so many other things.

If your target audience is in China or the Middle East, where the Seekers represent only 5% and 2% of the population, respectively, it won't be as much of a slam dunk. But you can pop the champagne corks if your target audience is in the United States (36%) or Central/South America (32%), where the archetype is far more dominant than the global average of 21%.

See how the murky gray is already creeping in? Depending on the markets you are operating in, what seems like a clear winner might be a loser or an even bigger winner than you thought.

BUCKLE UP; THERE'S MORE

Your target audience won't cleanly and precisely fit into one archetype because human beings are too complex to be pigeonholed like that. Most of us will have a dominant archetype but will also have a little of this and a little of that. We all have outlying traits that make us unique.

So of course when you group unique individuals into a target audience and try to describe that mass of people with a single archetype, it will be less than perfect. You can imagine how the combined nuances for all those unique individuals make everything a bit murky and gray.

BUT IT'S ALL FINE AND GOOD

All you are looking for is a signal in the noise that identifies what direction you should face. That's enough. That's several times better than what we do now, which is to randomly guess what to do based on something as ridiculous as age, gender, income, marital status, and so on.

And therein lies the whole point of this explanation: *it all depends.* That's the constant refrain I've had to learn to embrace since my work on valuegraphics began. Every time we look at the data for a target audience and search for the insights that will help our clients in the most powerful way possible, there's that unavoidable disclaimer: it depends.

Gary Vaynerchuk often comes up with pithy ways to explain things, and in this case, he wins the prize: "Content is king, but context is God."[24]

In our case, we might amend this to "Data is king, but context is God."

The Valuegraphics Archetype Quiz, the regional profile chapters, and the archetype chapters in this book will load you up with all kinds of data about your target audience. But until you apply what you know about your industry, the competitive environment you operate in, your brand positioning, the desired outcome you are looking for, the budget you have to work with, and so on—until you use those factors as a way to filter the data, it's only data. Your experience, knowledge, intuition, and gut feelings are what make data into actionable insights. The Values Thinking process we've outlined in the next chapter should help, but even that is only a guide to help you combine valuegraphic insights with what you already know to make better decisions.

But here's a win you can celebrate with 100% certainty.

---

24 Gary Vaynerchuk, "Content Is King, but Context Is God," 2016, https://www.garyvaynerchuk.com/content-is-king-but-context-is-god/

DAVID **ALLISON**

If you follow the steps in this book and use Values Thinking to make your decisions, your decisions will be based on what your target audience truly values. It's the most effective way to make decisions with the least amount of risk possible.

AN ADDITIONAL PERSPECTIVE

Let's close out this chapter with one last bit of the murky gray.

You've already read the regional profile chapters that apply to your geographic market area (Part Three), and so you've learned about the values of the population for your part of the world. In Part Five, you can compare those values to the archetype that is most applicable to your target audience. Combined, these two perspectives give you more information on your target audience than if you relied on only one viewpoint or the other.

It's like anything. Two perspectives on the same situation yield a far more robust understanding.

Think about a backyard BBQ.

One perspective comes from a drone camera hovering over the people you have gathered in your backyard. You can see that Sarah and Alex are facing each other, drinks in hand, in the middle of an animated conversation. Isn't it great to see your friends getting along? Oh, and in a back corner near the birdbath, you can see five kids sitting cross-legged in a circle, maybe playing cards. It's hard to tell. What a great day! So sunny!

The other perspective you have is from the back porch, with a gin and tonic in one hand, while the other hand shields your eyes from the sun. Sarah and Alex are actually in the middle of a fight. He ducks when she throws the contents of her glass at him. Then she pivots and storms away. And those kids? They are sitting in a circle passing around a beer they stole from the buffet table when the grown-ups weren't watching.

Both views of your summer backyard festivities are correct. Both are useful. Together, they give you a far better idea of what's going on.

CHAPTER 23

STEP FOUR: THE VALUES THINKING PROCESS

HERE IS THE MOST FREQUENT QUESTION I AM ASKED WHEN- ever we share the findings from a Valuegraphics Profile: "Wow, that's so cool! Love the insights, but what do we do now?"

I developed the Values Thinking process to answer that question. This is the "work" you need to do to operationalize the valuegraphics of your target audience. It's Step Four of the DIY Valuegraphics Toolkit, the process that brings it all together.

WHAT'S THE ISSUE?

> ## What's the issue?

As obvious as it may seem, the first thing you need to do is decide what you want to know.

Here are a few of the most common issues you could tackle with the Values Thinking process:

- Positioning a new brand or a brand extension
- Developing creative strategies for marketing campaigns
- Generating themes for social media content creation
- Creating promotional ideas to convert leads into customers
- Crafting sales language and pathing
- Planning customer journey touchpoints and principles
- Building loyalty program tiers and rewards
- Logic-checking brand extensions or new product concepts
- Prioritizing messages for your website
- Helping your customer service team customize their interactions with clients
- Designing UX strategies

The list of possible applications for the Values Thinking process is quite endless, and that's what makes it so useful. In fact, when I'm teaching organizations how to use the process, I'll often emphasize the universality of the process with the following exercise.

At the beginning of the workshop, before we even start talking about the Valuegraphics of the target audience, I break everyone up into small groups and send them away to brainstorm solutions to one (or, time permitting, both) of these questions:

1. You've invited your best customers to an event to thank them for their loyalty over the last year. What do you ask the catering company to prepare?

2. It's company policy to send your best customers a small gift during the holiday season. What should you send?

When the groups are done brainstorming, I have them quickly present their ideas. Then, at the end of the workshop, after learning how to use Values Thinking, I send everyone away again to answer the same questions. The ideas generated in the second go-around will have changed dramatically because they will be based on Values Thinking. This before-and-after perspective is a powerful way for everyone to see how Values Thinking makes even the smallest decisions better.

So grab a pen and a piece of paper and write down what your issue is. Then we can move on.

WHO ARE YOU TALKING TO?

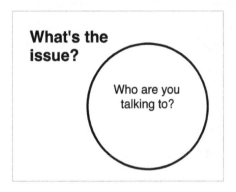

What's the issue?

Who are you talking to?

This is where demographics and psychographics come into play. But I have a monumental warning for you about the information you choose to include here: if it's not useful, leave it out. *If it doesn't help, it harms.*

Although that seems obvious, it's a piece of advice that many organizations unwittingly ignore.

You see, a decade or more ago, someone sent around a memo to the entire business world that said, "Data is the new gold." But what that cursed memo didn't explain is that *not all data is created equal.*

Data that can help you make smart decisions is absolutely as good as gold. But the rest of it, all the mountains of data that we've been collecting and piling up indiscriminately for far too long, isn't worth anything at all.

In fact, all that extraneous data is incredibly counterproductive. It is the primary cause of data paralysis, which is a fully preventable affliction I've seen far too often. The symptoms of data paralysis vary from one company to the next, but there is a common thread that connects them all.

They have so much data that they don't know what to do with it, which grinds everything to a halt because it feels like a problem that must be solved. Superfluous data is like a giant snowbank that organizations feel they must shovel through before getting on with things.

The solution is to wholeheartedly embrace selective attention. Ignore the data snowbank on the highway and drive around it. Leave it for someone else to clean up later, if at all. Someone on your team might be incredibly excited about the new data that analyzes your customers' pulse rates, eye movements, e-commerce habits, zip code demographics, or left shoe size. But unless it will help you make a decision about the issue you have on the table right at this very moment, forget about it. Keep calm and carry on.

For this step of the Values Thinking process, you need to examine the demographic data you have and, for example, decide if it matters that your target audience is male or female. If gender will not alter an actionable outcome, don't even put it on the table. There are certain products, services, and brands where income, age, gender, marital status, and so on might be important. Diapers will sell best to people who have kids; private jets will be more successful if you target the super rich; high-heeled shoes will tend to be more appealing to women. But unless your issue has something demographically limiting about it, demographics are irrelevant. They will only confuse everyone. So leave them out.

Let's be as critical about psychographic data, too. There are a billion definitions of the term "psychographics," and some of them go on for pages. The one I subscribe to is maybe the simplest: psychographics are a record of what has happened so far.

If the issue you are trying to address will benefit from some record of the past behaviors, feelings, emotions, or decisions of the target audience, then include it. It might be super relevant that these people own an average of 45 pairs of sneakers already if you are a sneaker company. It might be useful to know that the target audience you are focused on for this decision is full of angry people if the issue you are trying to solve is related to what they are mad about. But as with demographics, so, too, with psychographics: ignore whatever is useless.

Here's the best and simplest way to think about the information you need to collect for this step: *what's the least amount of data I need?* Academics refer to this perfect amount as optimum information load.

WHY DO THEY DO THINGS?

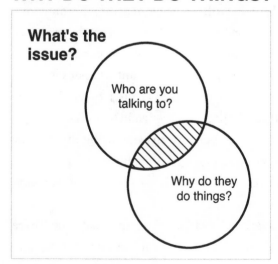

For one of two reasons, this is the step that we've historically skipped over in brainstorming. Either we didn't see how it was important, or we had some idea it was important but didn't have an accurate way to figure it out.

If you've read this far in the book, you already agree. You know that understanding the shared values of your target audience is mission critical if you hope to engage them and influence what they do. And now that you have the DIY tools in this book, you are all set to find out which values to include here.

For the issue at hand and for the target audience you've identified, what values will activate these people most effectively? You can think of these values using whatever metaphor you like: the buttons you need to push, the bells you need to ring, the magnets you need to activate, the musical notes you need to play.

HOW CAN YOU ENGAGE?

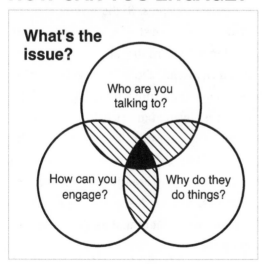

What's the issue?

Who are you talking to?

How can you engage?

Why do they do things?

The last step in the Values Thinking process is to anchor your thinking in reality.

I know, I know—I'm ruining all the fun. For decades, we've followed the golden rule of brainstorming, which states, "There are no silly ideas." But the fact is, there are Olympic-size swimming pools overflowing with an endless number of silly ideas.

We could exponentially boost sales of our new pickup truck overnight if we promised to refund 125% of the purchase price to anyone who was unhappy, with no questions asked. We could generate a lot of press coverage for our new energy drink if we paid Richard Branson to chug one back while dangling from a helicopter over a pit full of sharks. And it would be super amazing to hire one million micro-influencers to write social media posts extolling the virtue of our revolutionary new keto-macro-vegan-probiotic-soy-plant-protein supplement.

Those are extreme examples. Right? We all got the sarcasm there? Good. But if we start a Values Thinking brainstorming session with rules that allow anyone to say anything at all, it can yield a lot of ideas that will never fly.

Instead, let's encourage a more focused use of the Values Thinking process by including a list of what might be possible from a tactical perspective and then let the brilliant ideas fly based on those restrictions. Focused brainstorming is the goal. Every creative person I've ever met—writers, dancers, artists, designers—agrees that having some limiting parameters makes their creative output infinitely better.

It might help to think of this as using only "the tools you have for the job." Your tools will vary wildly depending on the issue, the audience, and other considerations like industry sector, competitive environment, and so on. All of which makes it hard for me to give you any guidance other than in the following very general way:

- What budget is allocated to address this issue and/ or what budget might be reallocated if the issue could be successfully addressed?

- Who will need to be sold on the idea internally before it gets a green light? What proof will they want that the solution is tenable? What success metrics will they be watching for?

- What human capital is available if the right solution surfaces? Who has capacity to execute on the idea and/or what might need to happen to create more capacity?

And if you'd rather talk like a regular human being instead of a business bot, ask yourself this:

- What can we afford?

- Who will need to be convinced?

- How much time can we devote to this?

LET THE VALUES THINKING BEGIN!

You are ready to go now. You know what the issue is. You have a concise description of who you are trying to reach.

You know what values will engage and influence them. And you know what you've got to work with.

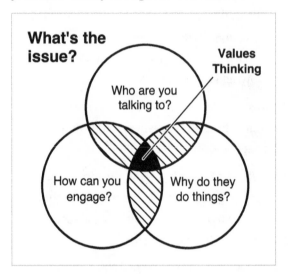

Start trying to solve the issue for those people with those values with the tools you have to work with.

How is this any different from normal old-fashioned brainstorming that we've all done before? Quite simply, you know what will work because you know what these people value.

Without valuegraphics for your target audience, you are not using Values Thinking. You are spitballing, guessing, blue-sky thinking, or whatever else you want to call it. You are looking for the proverbial needle in the haystack.

When you know the values your audience will respond to, you may still be looking for the needle in the haystack, but the haystack is exponentially smaller.

And if after all that, it still seems like the right idea to dangle Branson over a shark pit, I want to be there to see that. Send my invite to info@valuegraphics.com.

WHERE AND WHEN

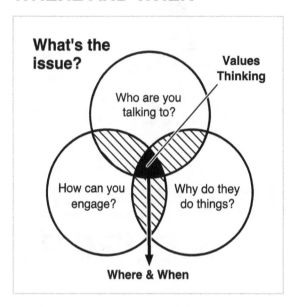

For this model to be complete, we must include a final step. After you've done all the smart work of developing those award-winning strategic ideas based on the values of your target audience, you need to figure out where you will use them and when.

This now moves the conversation firmly into the realm of project management, a realm that is rich and deep with experts. And my name is most definitely not among them.

CHAPTER 24

VALUES THINKING CASE STUDY: EDITION HOTELS IN EUROPE

WITH ALL DUE APOLOGIES TO WHOEVER HAS THIS JOB IN the real world, for the duration of this chapter I have taken on the role of Pretend Vice President (PVP) of Marketing for EDITION Hotels in Europe.

For this example of the DIY Valuegraphics Toolkit in action, I started by using the Valuegraphics Archetype Quiz to poll a target audience. Then I used the results to find my

Superhero Archetype, referenced the appropriate archetype chapter in this book, and compared what I found there to the applicable regional profile (also in this book). Finally, I used Values Thinking to tackle a burning question that had to be resolved.

As PVP, I don't have access to the EDITION customer database. So I had to make my own. I found 100 EDITION customers in the EU and sent them the Valuegraphics Archetype Quiz, but only if they:

- Stay at luxury hotels when they travel for work

- Choose EDITION as their favorite from a list of hotels

- Are extremely likely to stay at EDITION hotels again

THE VALUEGRAPHICS ARCHETYPE

After looking at the quiz results, we found that 43% of this customer group fit into the Workers archetype. So let's see what we know about them.

Turning to the Workers archetype in Chapter 29, we can see that the Workers in the EU are the second largest archetype for the region. This is a big and powerful archetype for me to ponder as I sip espresso from a tiny cup in my PVP marketing corner office at EDITON's corporate HQ.

Furthermore, we know that the Workers in the EU agree with each other 85% of the time on all 436 values, wants, needs, and expectations measured in the Valuegraphics

Database. That means I have an extremely cohesive group to focus on as I try to grow the market for EDITION in the region.

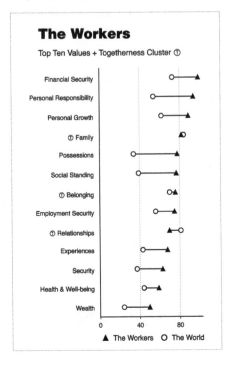

The Workers

Top Ten Values + Togetherness Cluster ⊤

The Workers are quite unique from the rest of the population, as is evident by the wide margins of difference between their top 10 values and the rankings of those same values elsewhere. But we like that because when we make decisions using this unique set of values as a North Star, we will carve out a distinct position in the market. It's not going to appeal to everyone, but for our customers, amplifying these values will make us incredibly magnetic.

Let's also take a look at the values for the entire population of the region as a more detailed comparison. I've built the following chart to make it easy to compare the Workers to the general population in our part of the world.

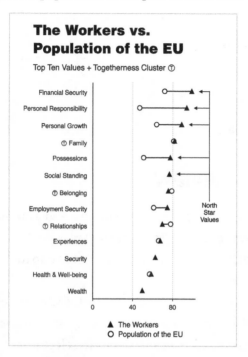

The Workers vs. Population of the EU

Top Ten Values + Togetherness Cluster ⑦

- ▲ The Workers
- ○ Population of the EU

Even though all the values in the top 10 list are powerful (remember, there are 56 in total and the rest did not make the cut), we need a simple set of values to use as North Star.

Now, the real VP Marketing of EDITION may have other ideas on what values are most applicable based on all kinds of other intelligence and experience I do not have. But as the PVP, I've arbitrarily chosen the top five where there is a juicy margin of difference between our Workers Archetype and everyone else in the market. We want to be unique and stand out from our competitors, but deciding *how* to stand out should be based on what our customers care about most.

So our list of North Star values for EDITION in the EU is as follows:

- Financial Security
- Personal Responsibility
- Personal Growth
- Possessions
- Social Standing

LET'S REVIEW

To recap what we've done so far, we asked a group of our customers to take the Valuegraphics Archetype Quiz. We discovered that 43% of that target market fit into the Workers Archetype.

Then we compared the values for the Workers to the values for the region where we are working—in this case, the EU.

This comparison allowed us to select a short list of values that are far more important to our workaholic customers than they are to everyone else.

If we use these values as a North Star to make decisions, we will be incredibly magnetic in a way that is unique to the target audience we want to activate.

NOW FOR SOME VALUES THINKING

Let's use what we've learned to answer a question that could be plaguing the VP of Marketing at EDITION right this minute. It certainly is weighing heavily on the PVP of Marketing as I write these words.

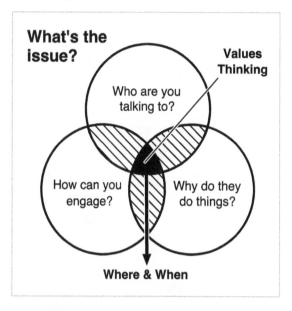

What's the Issue?

More and more, organizations are scrutinizing the travel choices made by executives who spend a lot of time on the road. How can EDITION help one of our most profitable customer segments (frequent business travelers) rationalize our above-market room rates to themselves and to anyone who might be asking? In other words, how do we solidify our base of support?

Who Are You Talking To?

Repeat customers who travel for work.

Why Do They Do Things?

The North Star values that we will use for this discussion are:

- Financial Security
- Personal Responsibility
- Personal Growth
- Possessions
- Social Standing

These are among the most powerful values for the target audience based on the archetype quiz and the regional valuegraphics. Our goal is to solve the issue using these values to influence the target audience.

How Can You Engage?

As PVP of Marketing, this is only one of the many objectives I need to accomplish, so I can't throw a lot of money at this. On the other hand, if I can lock down the patronage of this intensely profitable segment of the market, I'll be a rock star. So I could probably find a bit of money from somewhere if I had to. I'd like to stick to using social media messages, email, and perhaps a tasteful in-room message of some description. Of course, everything has to meet our contemporary luxury brand standards, too.

Values Thinking Ideas

After a review of our current initiatives and positioning at EDITION, I've found that we already align with the North

Star values for this target audience in many ways. We should amplify these however we can.

Here are some thought starters:

- **FINANCIAL SECURITY:** Falling short of your goals for a business trip could create a financial setback for your organization and for yourself. Today, you are on the road because vitally important work needs to be done face-to-face. Our properties and our teams understand this; we are focused on preparing you like a star athlete before the big game. Whatever you need from us, we will be standing by to deliver.

- **PERSONAL RESPONSIBILITY:** Our properties are set up as the ultimate business hub. You can work, work out, entertain, relax, and create meaningful new relationships in a setting that reflects the best of the local culture. Staying with us will maximize your time and your effort so you can accomplish more than you thought possible.

- **SOCIAL STANDING:** Our properties reflect well on you. Other luxury hotel brands are flashy, glitzy, and extravagant. We are quiet, refined, and simple.

Those three messages, prioritized and amplified through social media and email messaging, will drive home the point. Notably, we don't need to change anything about who we are or what we do in order to be more magnetic around those particular values.

What Else Could We Do?

For *Personal Growth*, we could add a free MasterClass sub-scription to the in-room entertainment options. When our business travelers are unwinding, they will appreciate tapping into some of the smartest minds in the world and learning new things.

What if we approached the MasterClass organization and asked them to co-brand a set of courses specifically for our business traveler guests, featuring topics that are of interest to them, taught by the world's best instructors on each subject? What if Martin Scorcese taught our guests how to make better social media videos for their organization? What if Barack Obama's former speechwriter taught executives how to craft a good speech? Of course, our fitness facilities will satisfy the need for *Personal Growth* for some of this target audience, too. We shouldn't forget the obvious.

And for Possessions?

Our successful business travelers do not need (and won't appreciate) logo-emblazoned ballcaps, pads, portfolio cases, and pens. Plus, we want to do something that addresses the specific issue on the table at the moment: rationalizing the premium we charge for our rooms in order to solidify our base.

Here's a thought. Ian Schrager, the world-renowned instigator of the boutique hotel concept, is the creative mastermind behind the EDITION hotel brand for Marriott. He is a tastemaker and an influencer who works on a global scale.

What if our loyalty program for business travelers featured a selection of merchandise curated by Ian Schrager and designed by architects responsible for our iconic properties? It's a great list that includes John Pawson, Yabu Pushelberg, Herzog and de Meuron, and a roll call of other incredibly well-known architects. There are also the famous contemporary artists in our collection, whose work is on display at our properties, who might be recruited for this project, too.

All told, there is an enormous and world-class creative brain trust associated with the brand that Ian Schrager could tap into, to make the loyalty reward program second to none. These designers and artists could be commissioned to create a series of objects and experiences exclusively for loyalty program members. These unique rewards would leverage the value of *Possessions* and, simultaneously, *Social Standing*. Plus, we'd be using aspects of our brand experience to reinforce how worthwhile our brand is. That circular reinforcement is always the best case, don't you think?

Where and When

Combined, these stories and initiatives would more than satisfy the North Star values for this target audience. It's time to get the project managers, copywriters, social media experts, and public relations teams on the case.

A robust social media content series would easily come from this. A few thoughtful emails to the appropriate customers in the database would be sure to generate interest. The website could have a feature on the landing page to highlight these touchpoints. And let's not forget, the

Schrager-curated rewards program involving such well-known names would most certainly be newsworthy. Call the PR team!

And would we have solved the issue? We'd have given these valuable customers the talking points they needed to rationalize our premium room rates, either to themselves or to anyone who might ask. That sounds like a mission accomplished to me.

A CLOSING THOUGHT

What would this exercise have looked like without Values Thinking?

It's hard to say, but it's safe to assume business travelers would be offered a business loyalty program focused on stereotypes of "what business travelers want." Usually, this is about access to a club floor lounge, with bland pastries and uninspiring drinks, along with a variety of room upgrades and other perks.

Those standard solutions might be effective, but they pale in comparison to the values-driven tactics designed to deliver exactly what this target audience cares about most. And in case someone from EDITION ends up reading this, imagine what we might find if we did a full custom profile using all the resources of the Valuegraphics Database. The insights we would identify would be as unique and powerful as each beautiful EDITION property.

THE 15 VALUEGRAPHICS ARCHETYPES

Instructions for Use

Using the archetype reference chapters is quite straight-forward. If, for example, you've arrived here armed with the knowledge that the Seekers are the archetype that works best for your target audience, you need to get yourself acquainted with Chapter 25.

- Each archetype chapter includes the shared values—the valuegraphics—of the people who make up the archetype and how important the archetype is across nine regions of the world.

- They also include contextual information that we've culled from the nearly 750,000 surveys in our benchmark dataset.

- To bring humanity back into these data-driven archetypes, we've included a selection of quotes from real people: things our survey respondents said to us that help paint a picture of who these people are and how they see the world.

Here's a tip: jot down any thoughts that occur to you as you read through each chapter. Those thoughts are bubbling up to the surface because your brain is trying to connect the dots between what you are learning and what you already know.

Scribble your notes in the margins or empty spaces in this book. You have my permission to write all over it! Nothing makes me happier than to see my books being used.

CHAPTER 25

ARCHETYPE: THE SEEKERS

GLOBAL RANKING: 1ST
Percentage of global population: 21%
Agreement on all 56 core human values: 85%

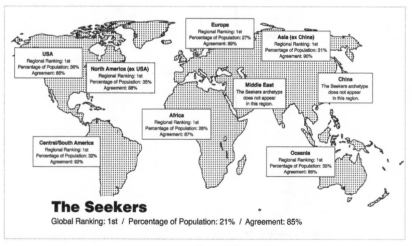

Europe
Regional Ranking: 1st
Percentage of Population: 27%
Agreement: 89%

Asia (ex China)
Regional Ranking: 1st
Percentage of Population: 31%
Agreement: 90%

USA
Regional Ranking: 1st
Percentage of Population: 36%
Agreement: 85%

North America (ex USA)
Regional Ranking: 1st
Percentage of Population: 35%
Agreement: 88%

China
The Seekers archetype
does not appear
in this region.

Middle East
The Seekers archetype
does not appear
in this region.

Africa
Regional Ranking: 1st
Percentage of Population: 26%
Agreement: 87%

Central/South America
Regional Ranking: 1st
Percentage of Population: 32%
Agreement: 92%

Oceania
Regional Ranking: 1st
Percentage of Population: 35%
Agreement: 88%

The Seekers
Global Ranking: 1st / Percentage of Population: 21% / Agreement: 85%

Where the Valuegraphics Archetype appears

This chart shows two things: the dominance of the archetype across the nine regions of the world and how often the people within the archetype agree with each other on the 56 core human values in the Valuegraphics Database.

WHAT MAKES THEM AN ARCHETYPE? The Unique Variable

The Seekers do not feel settled. In fact, they are unsettled, and they suspect it might be caused by any number of things. They all intend to move to a new home within the next two years, and some actually will.

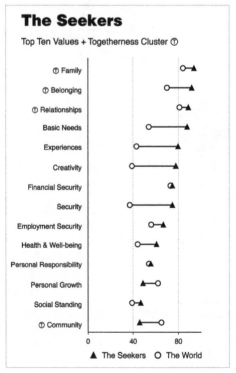

Archetype Valuegraphics Profile

From a possible 56 core human values, this chart compares the ranking of the top 10 values for the archetype to the same values for the population of the world. Also, since humans everywhere want to be with other humans, some of the five Togetherness Values will always appear. For definitions of the values, see Chapter 6.

ARCHETYPE CERTAINTIES

These things are true for at least 90% of the archetype:

- They move a lot.
- They have been renters for the majority of their adult lives.
- They are attracted to something unique and/or quirky about a home. It doesn't have to be expensive or exclusive, only different—although they will be frustrated by pointless features.
- They are open-minded about what a "home" is.
- They are uninterested in politics—even those that directly impact them.
- They are in debt.
- They rarely find comforts and luxuries important; they will primarily focus on meeting their *Basic Needs*. For some subgroups within the archetype, knowing their *Basic Needs* will be met for a significant period of time in advance will be seen as a luxury.
- They are big sports fans in North America, Europe,

and Oceania and big fans of community-based activities in Africa and the Middle East.

- They are attracted to doing things outside of the home, and not all of them will label/recognize these out-of-home activities as *Experiences*.

- They are not very good at sticking to budgets.

ARCHETYPE LIKELIHOODS

These things are true for 75%–89% of the archetype:

- They trend toward lower levels of education than the norm.

- They value *Creativity* more than all other archetypes, and they have the widest range of what they define as creative pursuits.

- They favor *Experiences* over *Possessions.*

- They have high levels of general anxiety.

- If they have *Loyalty*, they will be loyal only to those who are loyal to them.

- They are very likely to be foodies.

- They might be early adopters of technology, but they're not big users of that technology.

- They are attracted to diverse communities.

- They are unlikely, except in rare cases, to be environmentalists.

- They don't like wasted or redundant space in their homes.

FUN FACTS

The country with the largest percentage of the Seekers overall is Singapore, closely followed by the United States.

The country with the smallest percentage of the Seekers overall is Vietnam, followed by Italy and Korea.

There is no region or any country in any region where their number one value is anything other than *Family*, *Belonging*, or *Relationships*.

IN THEIR OWN WORDS:
Quotes from Survey Respondents

"I've got boxes of stuff I haven't unpacked for a decade because I'm never in one place long enough to bother."

"The world is huge and I want to live in as many parts of it as I can."

"I could improve the stability of my life. Sometimes I don't see where I'll be in five years and that scares me."

"Since I moved out for college, I've lived in 13 different places and never in one place for longer than a year."

CHAPTER 26

ARCHETYPE: THE FRUGAL

GLOBAL RANKING: 2ND

Percentage of global population: 17%

Agreement on all 56 core human values: 84%

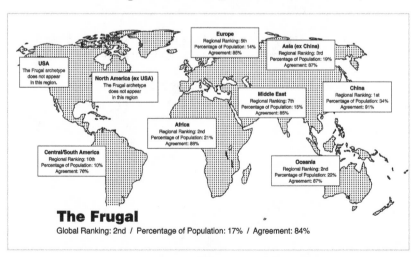

USA
The Frugal archetype does not appear in this region.

North America (ex USA)
The Frugal archetype does not appear in this region

Europe
Regional Ranking: 5th
Percentage of Population: 14%
Agreement: 85%

Asia (ex China)
Regional Ranking: 3rd
Percentage of Population: 19%
Agreement: 87%

China
Regional Ranking: 1st
Percentage of Population: 34%
Agreement: 91%

Middle East
Regional Ranking: 7th
Percentage of Population: 15%
Agreement: 85%

Africa
Regional Ranking: 2nd
Percentage of Population: 21%
Agreement: 88%

Central/South America
Regional Ranking: 10th
Percentage of Population: 10%
Agreement: 76%

Oceania
Regional Ranking: 2nd
Percentage of Population: 22%
Agreement: 87%

The Frugal
Global Ranking: 2nd / Percentage of Population: 17% / Agreement: 84%

Where the Valuegraphics Archetype appears

This chart shows two things: the dominance of the archetype across the nine regions of the world and how often the people within the archetype agree with each other on the 56 core human values in the Valuegraphics Database.

WHAT MAKES THEM AN ARCHETYPE: The Unique Variable

This group places an extreme level of importance on *Financial Security* because of the impact it has on their *Family*. The values of *Family* and *Financial Security* are inextricably linked. You might even think of them as one big value called *Family Financial Security*.

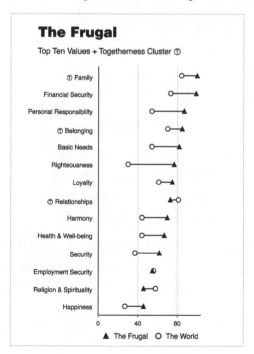

Archetype Valuegraphics Profile

From a possible 56 core human values, this chart compares the ranking of the top 10 values for the archetype to the same values for the population of the world. Also, since humans everywhere want to be with other humans, some of the five Togetherness Values will always appear. For definitions of the values, see Chapter 6.

ARCHETYPE CERTAINTIES

These things are true for at least 90% of the archetype:

- They believe *Financial Security* is about ensuring that their basic needs are met long term.
- They score humility as a strong personality trait.
- They avoid debt (unless the debt is absolutely necessary for their family).
- They are not early adopters; they are most likely to be followers.
- They are married with children.
- If their children are of adult age, then it is extremely likely they have provided them with something beyond the usual norms (e.g., a home or a down payment for one).
- A significant percentage of them struggled financially growing up and are determined that their children will not have to.

ARCHETYPE LIKELIHOODS

These things are true for 75%–89% of the archetype:

- If they have elderly parents, those parents are living with them (or a sibling).

- They feel secure with low/no debt.

- They are very habitual and have routine behaviors—for example, their daily schedules are carefully planned.

- They are politically conservative (in democratic countries).

- They make major decisions over time and in stages. First, they might decide to buy a car. Later, they decide what size of car. Later still, they settle on a brand. And so on.

FUN FACTS

This archetype shows up the most in China, followed by Indonesia and Fiji.

The Frugal tend to appear more in countries without a white majority. Accordingly, they don't appear in the United States or North America at all—only in Estonia and Greece in Europe and only in Pacific Island nations in Oceania. It is unclear why they do not appear in Central/South America.

IN THEIR OWN WORDS:
Quotes from Survey Respondents

"I work hard so my family can have a better life."

"Families can't thrive if they are worried about money."

"It is pure joy to be able to provide for my children and ensure they have all they need and want."

"As long as my family has what they need, I have what I need."

CHAPTER 27

ARCHETYPE: THE CREATIVES

GLOBAL RANKING: 3RD

Percentage of global population: 12%

Agreement on all 56 core human values: 81%

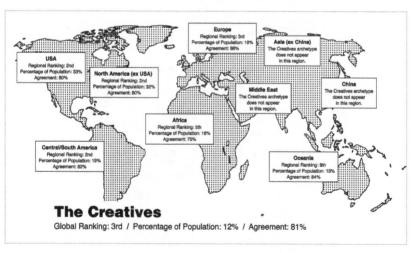

The Creatives

Global Ranking: 3rd / Percentage of Population: 12% / Agreement: 81%

Where the Valuegraphics Archetype appears

This chart shows two things: the dominance of the archetype across the nine regions of the world and how often the people within the archetype agree with each other on the 56 core human values in the Valuegraphics Database.

WHAT MAKES THEM AN ARCHETYPE: The Unique Variable

Members of this archetype consider *Creativity* to be at least somewhat important in their lives, and they spend a minimum of five hours (usually much more) per week being creative.

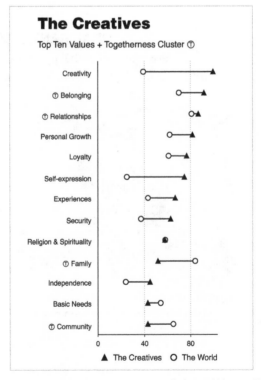

Archetype Valuegraphics Profile

From a possible 56 core human values, this chart compares the ranking of the top 10 values for the archetype to the same values for the population of the world. Also, since humans everywhere want to be with other humans, some of the five Togetherness Values will always appear. For definitions of the values, see Chapter 6.

ARCHETYPE CERTAINTIES

These things are true for at least 90% of the archetype:

- They are frustrated by boredom.
- They are self-employed or working multiple jobs.
- They are in some debt.
- They are highly emotionally aware.
- They reject most mainstream culture (e.g., sports).
- They are very attracted to supporting the little guy (e.g., local businesses, other creatives).
- If their *Creativity* is part of their work, then they are extremely likely to have another creative outlet that isn't work related.

ARCHETYPE LIKELIHOODS

These things are true for 75%–89% of the archetype:

- If they have kids, they are less involved with their children compared to other parents.
- They are always looking for ways to improve their lives.

- They avoid confrontation.

- They enjoy seeing other creative people emerging (e.g., new artists) and are unlikely to be threatened by the competition.

- They are on the hunt for new experiences all the time unless it has to do with their specific creative outlet, in which case they want more and more of the same experiences.

FUN FACTS

This archetype doesn't appear in China or the Middle East. In fact, the core value of *Creativity* doesn't appear in the top 25 values for either region.

The country with the largest appearance of *Creativity* overall is Australia, closely followed by the United States, Canada, and the Netherlands.

They do not want to be sold creative products and services. They want to be the creators. They will buy products and services that support their journey.

In all valuegraphics research, survey respondents are free to define what the value means. In other words, there are as many different definitions of *Creativity* as there are flavors of ice cream.

IN THEIR OWN WORDS:
Quotes from Survey Respondents

"Having a creative outlet is extremely important to me. I spend a lot of time doing my thing!"

"Being consciously creative gets me through many situations."

"Being creative gives me opportunities to express who I am and explore who I am."

"I guess this dates way back to when I was growing up and my parents would encourage us all to try new things. Later in life, being creative became an emotional outlet for me."

CHAPTER 28

ARCHETYPE: THE LOYALISTS

GLOBAL RANKING: 5TH

Percentage of global population: 12%

Agreement on all 56 core human values: 82%

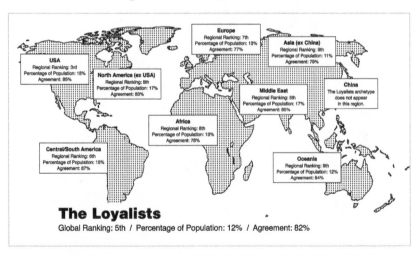

USA
Regional Ranking: 3rd
Percentage of Population: 15%
Agreement: 85%

North America (ex USA)
Regional Ranking: 5th
Percentage of Population: 17%
Agreement: 83%

Europe
Regional Ranking: 7th
Percentage of Population: 13%
Agreement: 77%

Asia (ex China)
Regional Ranking: 9th
Percentage of Population: 11%
Agreement: 79%

China
The Loyalists archetype
does not appear
in this region.

Middle East
Regional Ranking: 5th
Percentage of Population: 17%
Agreement: 85%

Africa
Regional Ranking: 8th
Percentage of Population: 13%
Agreement: 78%

Central/South America
Regional Ranking: 6th
Percentage of Population: 15%
Agreement: 87%

Oceania
Regional Ranking: 9th
Percentage of Population: 12%
Agreement: 84%

The Loyalists

Global Ranking: 5th / Percentage of Population: 12% / Agreement: 82%

Where the Valuegraphics Archetype appears

This chart shows two things: the dominance of the archetype across the nine regions of the world and how often the people within the archetype agree with each other on the 56 core human values in the Valuegraphics Database.

WHAT MAKES THEM AN ARCHETYPE: The Unique Variable

Members of this archetype are driven by *Loyalty*, and it often begins with a decision that someone or something has earned their loyalty. Once Loyalists are engaged, it's hard to lose them. They'll forgive minor transgressions and remain loyal through thick and thin.

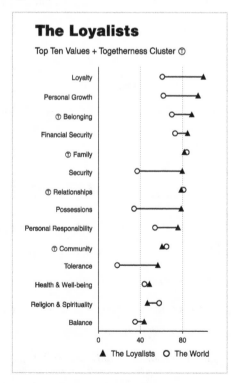

Archetype Valuegraphics Profile

From a possible 56 core human values, this chart compares the ranking of the top 10 values for the archetype to the same values for the population of the world. Also, since humans everywhere want to be with other humans, some of the five Togetherness Values will always appear. For definitions of the values, see Chapter 6.

ARCHETYPE CERTAINTIES

These things are true for at least 90% of the archetype:

- They are not big fans of change or even accomplishment (as that would be a kind of change).

- They embrace some form of religion or spirituality.

- They tend to be married more than the norm.

- They have an altruistic side.

- They are collectors of something.

- Their life is lived according to some form of routine.

- They are very people-centric.

ARCHETYPE LIKELIHOODS

These things are true for 75%–89% of the archetype:

- They are TV watchers and series bingers.

- They are attracted to authenticity in others.

- They seek *Financial Security* about covering the basic expenses over the long term.

- They believe *Personal Growth* is about expanding

their current skills, as opposed to growth in new ways.

FUN FACTS

The largest appearance of the Loyalists overall is in Norway.

The Loyalists do not appear in China, Peru, Malaysia, or the Cook Islands.

Although the Loyalist archetype doesn't appear in certain countries, those countries still rank *Loyalty* as a value. In Peru, as an example, *Loyalty* is tied up with morals rather than a specific set of behaviors that would qualify for membership in this archetype.

IN THEIR OWN WORDS:
Quotes from Survey Respondents

"I'm very driven by routine and that means going to the same people who help me repeatedly."

"I'm loyal to those who show me they value my loyalty."

"I'm much more likely to return to a company I have interacted with before if they provided great service than I am to go somewhere new, even if this means traveling."

"If you want loyalty from others, you need to show it to them. I know that's potentially a paradox, but it has to start with someone."

CHAPTER 29

ARCHETYPE: THE WORKERS

GLOBAL RANKING: 5TH

Percentage of global population: 12%

Agreement on all 56 core human values: 82%

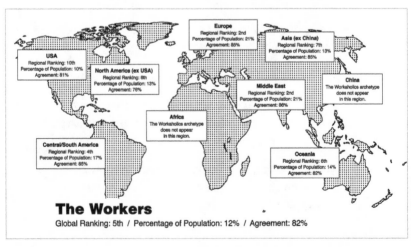

Europe
Regional Ranking: 2nd
Percentage of Population: 21%
Agreement: 85%

Asia (ex China)
Regional Ranking: 7th
Percentage of Population: 13%
Agreement: 85%

USA
Regional Ranking: 10th
Percentage of Population: 10%
Agreement: 81%

North America (ex USA)
Regional Ranking: 8th
Percentage of Population: 13%
Agreement: 76%

China
The Workaholics archetype
does not appear
in this region.

Middle East
Regional Ranking: 2nd
Percentage of Population: 21%
Agreement: 86%

Africa
The Workaholics archetype
does not appear
in this region.

Central/South America
Regional Ranking: 4th
Percentage of Population: 17%
Agreement: 85%

Oceania
Regional Ranking: 8th
Percentage of Population: 14%
Agreement: 82%

The Workers
Global Ranking: 5th / Percentage of Population: 12% / Agreement: 82%

Where the Valuegraphics Archetype appears

This chart shows two things: the dominance of the archetype across the nine regions of the world and how often the people within the archetype agree with each other on the 56 core human values in the Valuegraphics Database.

WHAT MAKES THEM AN ARCHETYPE: The Unique Variable

The Workers are motivated by some specific reason to work at least 80 hours per week. The motivating factor might be their career ambitions or their family. We also see specific profiles where the motivating factor is some other life-related goal, such as earning a degree, taking a sabbatical from work, or buying a second (or third!) home.

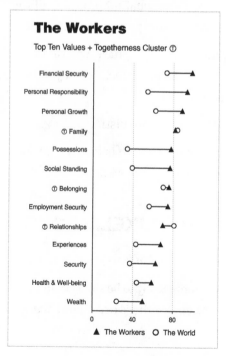

Archetype Valuegraphics Profile

From a possible 56 core human values, this chart compares the ranking of the top 10 values for the archetype to the same values for the population of the world. Also, since humans everywhere want to be with other humans, some of the five Togetherness Values will always appear. For definitions of the values, see Chapter 6.

ARCHETYPE CERTAINTIES

These things are true for at least 90% of the archetype:

- They work 80+ hours per week.

- They are chasing promotions and will do what's required to get them.

- They care about what others think of them and network only to improve their prospects.

- They more than likely have a private school education and a formal education beyond an undergraduate degree.

- They are not very altruistic.

- Their *Personal Growth* is focused on something that advances their work.

ARCHETYPE LIKELIHOODS

These things are true for 75%–89% of the archetype:

- They are more likely to be single than other archetypes (except for those driven by *Family*).

- They are working (or have worked) in the same or similar industry to a parent.
- They are very proud of their accomplishments.
- They hate wasting time.
- They are early adopters of technology.

FUN FACTS

The country with the most Workers is Turkey.

The country with the most Workers who are motivated by their career is South Korea.

The country with the most Workers motivated by other life goals is Mexico.

France has the most Workers motivated by *Creativity*.

Workers motivated by *Family* appear most in Norway.

IN THEIR OWN WORDS: Quotes from Survey Respondents

"I know what I want in life and getting there means focusing on my career over anything else."

"Life is expensive. Having a family is expensive. Both require someone to work hard and that someone is me."

"My career is important to me, and I'll live at the office if that's the only way to continue up the ladder."

"Money opens doors; miracles hide behind those doors."

"People have high expectations of me and that makes me work hard to meet those expectations."

CHAPTER 30

ARCHETYPE: THE SAVERS

GLOBAL RANKING: 6TH

Percentage of global population: 12%

Agreement on all 56 core human values: 81%

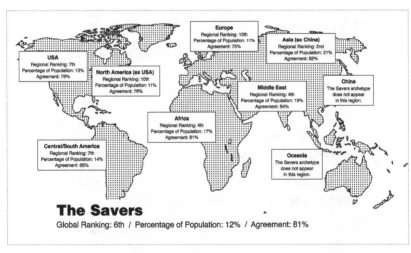

Europe
Regional Ranking: 10th
Percentage of Population: 11%
Agreement: 75%

Asia (ex China)
Regional Ranking: 2nd
Percentage of Population: 21%
Agreement: 82%

USA
Regional Ranking: 7th
Percentage of Population: 13%
Agreement: 76%

North America (ex USA)
Regional Ranking: 10th
Percentage of Population: 11%
Agreement: 76%

China
The Savers archetype
does not appear
in this region.

Middle East
Regional Ranking: 4th
Percentage of Population: 19%
Agreement: 84%

Africa
Regional Ranking: 4th
Percentage of Population: 17%
Agreement: 81%

Central/South America
Regional Ranking: 7th
Percentage of Population: 14%
Agreement: 85%

Oceania
The Savers archetype
does not appear
in this region.

The Savers

Global Ranking: 6th / Percentage of Population: 12% / Agreement: 81%

Where the Valuegraphics Archetype appears

This chart shows two things: the dominance of the archetype across the nine regions of the world and how often the people within the archetype agree with each other on the 56 core human values in the Valuegraphics Database.

WHAT MAKES THEM AN ARCHETYPE: The Unique Variable

Members of this archetype avoid debt at all costs and like to accumulate whatever they can.

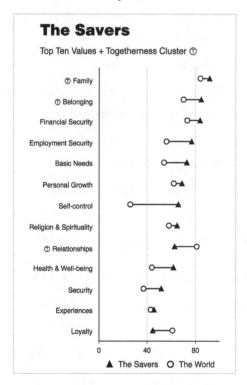

Archetype Valuegraphics Profile

From a possible 56 core human values, this chart compares the ranking of the top 10 values for the archetype to the same values for the population of the world. Also, since humans everywhere want to be with other humans, some of the five Togetherness Values will always appear. For definitions of the values, see Chapter 6.

ARCHETYPE CERTAINTIES

These things are true for at least 90% of the archetype:

- They are attracted to *Possessions* but will not go into debt to get them.

- They are not early adopters.

- They are married or in a committed relationship and are parents of dependent children.

- They plan ahead and have one eye on some version of retirement or semi-retirement.

- They will take on debt for education.

ARCHETYPE LIKELIHOODS

These things are true for 75%–89% of the archetype:

- Before any major purchase decision, they consider the impact it will have on their future.

- Their saving is motivated by feeling secure.

- They expect their children to pay/borrow for their own education.

- They attend some form of church service regularly.

- They like wine.

- Their *Health & Well-Being* is connected to feeling secure financially and physically.

- They enjoy "doing without" things because the self-control and sacrifice required is connected to their future security. The act of saying no to themselves is also seen as a kind of *Personal Growth*.

- They love establishing and sticking to routines.

FUN FACTS

The largest appearance of the Savers overall is in Japan.

Although the Savers do not appear in China or Oceania, *Financial Security* still ranks highly, suggesting the values and traits of the Savers are present in other forms.

The Savers do not appear as an archetype in Sudan, Uzbekistan, Pakistan, or Bhutan.

IN THEIR OWN WORDS: Quotes from Survey Respondents

"I pride myself on my routine."

"Being sensible with money makes me content."

"I strive now to thrive later."

"If I want something, I'll save tightly to get it, but I will get it."

"I'm attracted more to quality and durability than what is trendy or name brands."

"We always research our options before making a major purchase, and we expect to find the information we want or we move on."

CHAPTER 31

ARCHETYPE: THE HARMONIOUS

GLOBAL RANKING: 7TH

Percentage of global population: 10%

Agreement on all 56 core human values: 86%

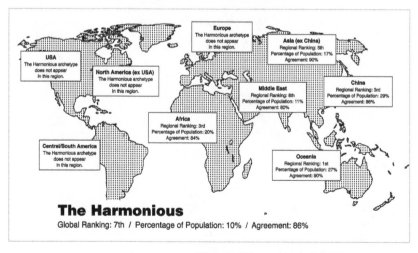

The Harmonious

Global Ranking: 7th / Percentage of Population: 10% / Agreement: 86%

Where the Valuegraphics Archetype appears

This chart shows two things: the dominance of the archetype across the nine regions of the world and how often the people within the archetype agree with each other on the 56 core human values in the Valuegraphics Database.

WHAT MAKES THEM AN ARCHETYPE: The Unique Variable

This group seeks *Harmony* because of the benefit it has for *Family* and within their family. These two values are so closely intertwined that they might be thought of as one *Family Harmony* value.

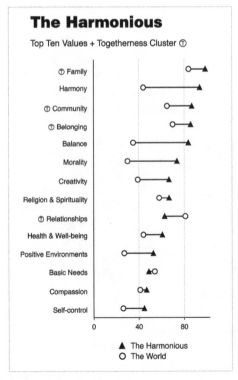

Archetype Valuegraphics Profile

From a possible 56 core human values, this chart compares the ranking of the top 10 values for the archetype to the same values for the population of the world. Also, since humans everywhere want to be with other humans, some of the five Togetherness Values will always appear. For definitions of the values, see Chapter 6.

ARCHETYPE CERTAINTIES

These things are true for at least 90% of the archetype:

- They define *Harmony* as a balance within the family and/or the community.

- They are married with children.

- They have some formal education.

- They are uninterested in politics unless it threatens Family.

- Their extended family is included in how they view the value of Family.

- They engage in *Creativity* with their family members.

ARCHETYPE LIKELIHOODS

These things are true for 75%–89% of the archetype:

- *Religion & Spirituality* and *Health & Well-Being* are interconnected.

- *Morality* isn't something they have to think about. In fact, it is so integrated in their lives that they have a hard time describing it.

- Although *Personal Responsibility* does not appear in the top 10, they feel a strong sense of responsibility to their family and/or community.
- They connect *Creativity* to individualism.

FUN FACTS

This archetype tends to appear more in countries without a white majority. Accordingly, it doesn't appear in the United States, Canada, or North America at all. It only appears in Estonia and Greece in Europe and only in Pacific Island nations in Oceania. It is unclear why it does not appear in Central/South America.

IN THEIR OWN WORDS:
Quotes from Survey Respondents

"A peaceful life is a blessing for my family."

"If one in the family is struggling, we are all struggling."

"It doesn't matter what is happening outside of the home as long as my children feel safe within it."

"Any decision I make or any purchase I make must pass the test of being good for my family."

"I tire of the individualistic advertising we get punished with every day. We are not individuals. We are members of collectives, and my purchase decisions reflect this."

"I prefer to buy local because my money helps families of local people."

"Don't tell me how to do something; tell me how something will make me feel."

CHAPTER 32

ARCHETYPE: THE ENVIRON- MENTALS

GLOBAL RANKING: 8TH

Percentage of global population: 9%

Agreement on all 56 core human values: 82%

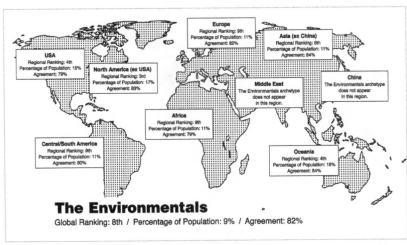

Europe
Regional Ranking: 9th
Percentage of Population: 11%
Agreement: 82%

Asia (ex China)
Regional Ranking: 8th
Percentage of Population: 11%
Agreement: 84%

USA
Regional Ranking: 4th
Percentage of Population: 15%
Agreement: 79%

North America (ex USA)
Regional Ranking: 3rd
Percentage of Population: 17%
Agreement: 83%

Middle East
The Environmentals archetype does not appear in this region.

China
The Environmentals archetype does not appear in this region.

Africa
Regional Ranking: 9th
Percentage of Population: 11%
Agreement: 79%

Central/South America
Regional Ranking: 9th
Percentage of Population: 11%
Agreement: 80%

Oceania
Regional Ranking: 4th
Percentage of Population: 18%
Agreement: 84%

The Environmentals
Global Ranking: 8th / Percentage of Population: 9% / Agreement: 82%

Where the Valuegraphics Archetype appears

This chart shows two things: the dominance of the archetype across the nine regions of the world and how often the people within the archetype agree with each other on the 56 core human values in the Valuegraphics Database.

WHAT MAKES THEM AN ARCHETYPE: The Unique Variable

Members of this archetype share a concern for the environment and are motivated to improve it. They are keenly aware of both the impact they have on their environment and the impact their environment has on them.

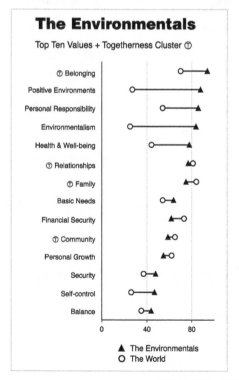

Archetype Valuegraphics Profile

From a possible 56 core human values, this chart compares the ranking of the top 10 values for the archetype to the same values for the population of the world. Also, since humans everywhere want to be with other humans, some of the five Togetherness Values will always appear. For definitions of the values, see Chapter 6.

ARCHETYPE CERTAINTIES

These things are true for at least 90% of the archetype:

- They have family money.
- Their levels of debt are lower than the norm.
- They grow some of their own food.
- They are attracted to forms of spirituality—e.g., meditation—but not formal religions.
- They are highly educated, in some cases self-taught.
- They are light social media users.
- They are big recyclers—will even collect other people's recycling.
- They are aware of the impact of their actions on the planet.

ARCHETYPE LIKELIHOODS

These things are true for 75%–89% of the archetype:

- They don't support a major political party.

- They prioritize what they describe as "clean living."

- They are aware of their own culture.

- They have high emotional awareness.

- They perceive technology as having a part to play in saving the environment.

- They define *Health & Well-Being* in a holistic way.

- They are attracted to evidence-based actions.

- They may carry some guilt from their actions; they know they could be doing better.

FUN FACTS

The Environmentals fall into one of two camps. The Personal Environmentals are focused on the environments that they are part of, while the Collective Environmentals are more motivated by group action on large-scale issues that impact the planet overall.

The largest appearances of the Environmentals are in Switzerland, Austria, and Canada.

The largest appearance of the Personal Environmentals is in Denmark.

The largest appearance of the Collective Environmentals is in New Zealand and Australia.

Countries with no Environmentals include South Africa, Ghana, Wales, and Mexico.

Turkey is the only country in the Middle East where the Environmentals appear.

IN THEIR OWN WORDS:
Quotes from Survey Respondents

"We are part of the environment and the environment is part of us. We are one."

"I feel so pure when I spend time in nature and go through withdrawals when I don't."

"I try to offset the bad I do to the environment with a double-good."

"I left the city so my family could live surrounded by clean air. We miss out on a lot by living rural, but the benefits outweigh that loss."

"For me, it's about more than caring about the environment and it is about being one with it, so I selected this value over Environmentalism. I'm not an environmentalist; I'm just a person who appreciates grass over concrete."

"Those who really care about the environment see right through the brands who pretend to care."

CHAPTER 33

ARCHETYPE: THE ADVENTURERS

GLOBAL RANKING: 7TH

Percentage of global population: 10%

Agreement on all 56 core human values: 86%

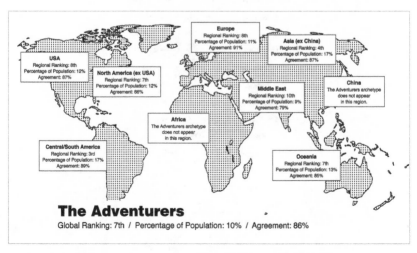

Europe
Regional Ranking: 8th
Percentage of Population: 11%
Agreement: 91%

Asia (ex China)
Regional Ranking: 4th
Percentage of Population: 17%
Agreement: 87%

USA
Regional Ranking: 8th
Percentage of Population: 12%
Agreement: 87%

North America (ex USA)
Regional Ranking: 7th
Percentage of Population: 12%
Agreement: 86%

China
The Adventurers archetype does not appear in this region.

Middle East
Regional Ranking: 10th
Percentage of Population: 9%
Agreement: 79%

Africa
The Adventurers archetype does not appear in this region.

Central/South America
Regional Ranking: 3rd
Percentage of Population: 17%
Agreement: 89%

Oceania
Regional Ranking: 7th
Percentage of Population: 13%
Agreement: 85%

The Adventurers
Global Ranking: 7th / Percentage of Population: 10% / Agreement: 86%

Where the Valuegraphics Archetype appears

This chart shows two things: the dominance of the archetype across the nine regions of the world and how often the people within the archetype agree with each other on the 56 core human values in the Valuegraphics Database.

WHAT MAKES THEM AN ARCHE TYPE: The Unique Variable

Members of this archetype are motivated by *Experiences* over anything else. Confusingly, sometimes they see acquisition of objects as an experience (buying a home is an experience), and sometimes they see experiences as a thing they can keep (a fantasy vacation is a memory to be treasured). Tread cautiously here!

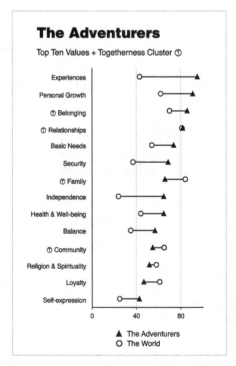

The Adventurers

Top Ten Values + Togetherness Cluster ⊤

Archetype Valuegraphics Profile

DAVID **ALLISON**

From a possible 56 core human values, this chart compares the ranking of the top 10 values for the archetype to the same values for the population of the world. Also, since humans everywhere want to be with other humans, some of the five Togetherness Values will always appear. For definitions of the values, see Chapter 6.

ARCHETYPE CERTAINTIES

These things are true for at least 90% of the archetype:

- They have lived in more locations than the norm.

- They will not do without the *Experiences* they crave even if it means taking on debt.

- Their *Health & Well-Being* includes mental, emotional, and physical definitions.

- They are unconcerned about their quality of life; possessions are of little concern.

- They are keen self-educators; they see education as a form of *Personal Growth.*

- They have high awareness of their impact on the environment and the places they visit.

ARCHETYPE LIKELIHOODS

These things are true for 75%–89% of the archetype:

- They intensely focus on their career in bursts in order to fund/make possible their next big experience.

- They spend at least three nights a week out.

- They are not religious but will enjoy religious experiences (e.g., visiting temples or shrines).

- They don't consider quality a factor in most decisions (e.g., they will stay in a terrible accommodation if it makes a new experience possible).

- They are attracted to some experiences because they are a form of *Personal Growth.*

- They save their money between adventures so the next experience can be sooner.

FUN FACTS

The largest appearance of the Adventurers is in the Netherlands.

The Adventurers do not appear at all in Turkey, Iceland, Togo, Morocco, and Israel.

Certain values will be heightened and more dominant while in the middle of an adventure and quieter in between (e.g., *Personal Growth* would be high while trekking in the Amazon forest, but *Basic Needs* would be higher while saving up for that trip). This is true in other Valuegraphics Profiles, but it's especially strong for this archetype.

IN THEIR OWN WORDS:
Quotes from Survey Respondents

"I'd prefer to go somewhere new than get a promotion."

"Success for me is learning a new skill, not having a large bank balance."

"Do what you've always done and you'll get what you've always gotten. No, thanks."

"I want to extend my comfort zones beyond where they currently are."

"One of life's simple pleasures is a Sunday adventure with my family to somewhere new or somewhere we all love."

"I'll stick with a brand if I have enjoyed the experience of using their products in the past."

"Sure, the adrenaline is great, but how much you learn about yourself by doing something challenging is what lasts."

CHAPTER 34

ARCHETYPE: THE ANTI-MATERIALISTS

GLOBAL RANKING: 9TH

Percentage of global population: 8%

Agreement on all 56 core human values: 81%

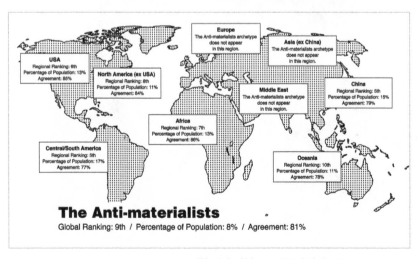

Where the Valuegraphics Archetype appears

This chart shows two things: the dominance of the archetype across the nine regions of the world and how often the people within the archetype agree with each other on the 56 core human values in the Valuegraphics Database.

WHAT MAKES THEM AN ARCHETYPE: The Unique Variable

In various ways and to varying degrees, members of this archetype reject material possessions.

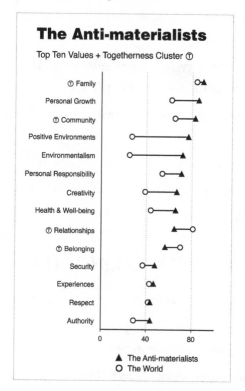

The Anti-materialists

Top Ten Values + Togetherness Cluster ⓣ

① Family
Personal Growth
① Community
Positive Environments
Environmentalism
Personal Responsibility
Creativity
Health & Well-being
① Relationships
① Belonging
Security
Experiences
Respect
Authority

0   40   80

▲ The Anti-materialists
O The World

Archetype Valuegraphics Profile

From a possible 56 core human values, this chart compares the ranking of the top 10 values for the archetype to the same values for the population of the world. Also, since humans everywhere want to be with other humans, some of the five Togetherness Values will always appear. For definitions of the values, see Chapter 6.

ARCHETYPE CERTAINTIES

These things are true for at least 90% of the archetype:

- The importance of *Possessions* is extremely low or nonexistent.

- Their memories are important to them. They think fondly of the past and of their ancestors.

- They are aware of their environmental impact.

- They will self-educate or enroll for continuing education on topics of interest to them.

- Although they don't seek out new possessions, they do value what they have.

ARCHETYPE LIKELIHOODS

These things are true for 75%–89% of the archetype:

- They are not early adopters of technology (most likely to be late adopters or even laggards).

- They are concerned about the environment.

- They will collect something that relates to a treasured memory (e.g., stamps because their grandfather did).

- They consider reusing products to be a form of *Creativity*.

- They have strong family ties to their local area.

- They are conservative politically (in democratic countries).

FUN FACTS

The largest appearance of the Anti-materialists is in Chile.

In addition to the three regions where the Anti-materialists don't appear—i.e., Europe, Asia (ex China), and the Middle East—they're also absent in Brazil, Turkey, and Mexico.

IN THEIR OWN WORDS:
Quotes from Survey Respondents

"Having things doesn't interest me. Living life does."

"I have the same car I bought as a teenager. It's not fancy, but it does what a car needs to do."

"The more possessions I have, the more I feel weighed down."

"What I want and what I need are the same thing."

"I appreciate when a business advertises their product or service with practicality at the center. I'm not a dog and I don't get excited at buzzwords. I get excited when I can do something more efficiently."

CHAPTER 35

ARCHETYPE: THE STEADY

GLOBAL RANKING: 11TH

Percentage of global population: 7%

Agreement on all 56 core human values: 79%

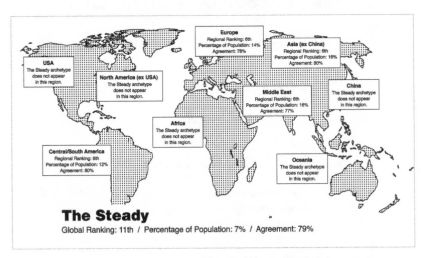

The Steady

Global Ranking: 11th / Percentage of Population: 7% / Agreement: 79%

Where the Valuegraphics Archetype appears

This chart shows two things: the dominance of the archetype across the nine regions of the world and how often the people within the archetype agree with each other on the 56 core human values in the Valuegraphics Database.

WHAT MAKES THEM AN ARCHETYPE: The Unique Variable

The Steady are conservative in all things, especially when it comes to the social aspects of their life. They aren't risk takers; they avoid change, and they like things to stay the way they are. They live a traditional family life and believe in good morals.

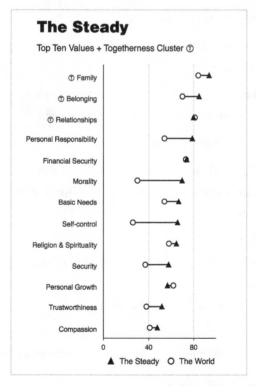

Archetype Valuegraphics Profile

From a possible 56 core human values, this chart compares the ranking of the top 10 values for the archetype to the same values for the population of the world. Also, since humans everywhere want to be with other humans, some of the five Togetherness Values will always appear. For definitions of the values, see Chapter 6.

ARCHETYPE CERTAINTIES

These things are true for at least 90% of the archetype:

- They are calculated decision-makers—they're extremely unlikely to take risks.

- They are very traditional.

- They are very social but only within small, tight-knit circles.

- They are at least somewhat likely to have lived in the same town or city their entire lives.

- They live life according to a plan.

- They will take on debt for a justifiable reason (home, car, education, etc.), but the risk will be calculated and they will pay off debts before they are due.

- They are married with children and have strong family ties; if they are younger, then they seek marriage and plan to have children.

- In some regions, the ways that these conservative values manifest may be seen as outdated by outsiders (e.g., gender equality).

ARCHETYPE LIKELIHOODS

These things are true for 75%–89% of the archetype:

- They rarely attend large social gatherings and events (e.g., concerts, sporting events).

- They will have inherited something from their parents who were also from this archetype (e.g., a home or other assets).

- They will have or have had a parent living with them.

- They believe in children going out into the world and experiencing life early.

FUN FACTS

The largest appearance of the Steady is in Saudi Arabia, Pakistan, and Lebanon. The archetype does not appear in Mauritius, Namibia, Colombia, or the Philippines. Although the archetype does not appear in the United States or elsewhere in North America, we do see similar profiles. But they are not dominant enough to be archetypes.

IN THEIR OWN WORDS:
Quotes from Survey Respondents

"I do what I've gotta do when I've gotta do it."

"I avoid taking risks, or if I have to take one, I will plan for it and understand all of my options."

"Risk taking is for other people, not me."

"I take my responsibilities seriously and get frustrated by those who do not."

"My father taught me to meet my responsibilities first and then have fun but never have so much fun that I can't meet my responsibilities the next time they come around."

"I don't like when I go to one of my favorite shops and they've changed something around."

"I will keep taking my business to a local establishment that shows traditional values and treats their customers with respect."

"I've been taking my family to the same vacation spot for years, and it is the same spot my parents took us. I love sharing the history of the place with my children and hope they will do the same with theirs."

CHAPTER 36

ARCHETYPE: THE MORAL

GLOBAL RANKING: 12TH

Percentage of global population: 6%

Agreement on all 56 core human values: 76%

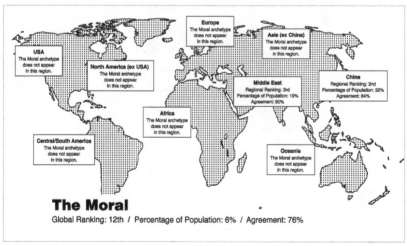

The Moral

Global Ranking: 12th / Percentage of Population: 6% / Agreement: 76%

Where the Valuegraphics Archetype appears

This chart shows two things: the dominance of the archetype across the nine regions of the world and how often the people within the archetype agree with each other on the 56 core human values in the Valuegraphics Database.

WHAT MAKES THEM AN ARCHETYPE: The Unique Variable

Righteousness ranks more highly here than any other archetype, and it's so closely intertwined with *Family* as to be almost one value—you might call it *Family Righteousness*. The definition of *Righteousness* varies but can be summed up by applying the word "moral," which we are using as a kind of shorthand for honesty, integrity, goodness, and perhaps most importantly, an ability to justify one's actions as being good.

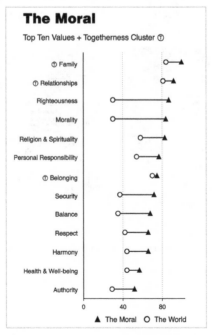

Archetype Valuegraphics Profile

From a possible 56 core human values, this chart compares the ranking of the top 10 values for the archetype to the same values for the population of the world. Also, since humans everywhere want to be with other humans, some of the five Togetherness Values will always appear. For definitions of the values, see Chapter 6.

ARCHETYPE CERTAINTIES

These things are true for at least 90% of the archetype:

- They value the importance of honesty and integrity as it relates to protecting the family name and reputation.

- They have a rich family history that they are trying to protect and uphold.

- They are strict parents and harsh on those who don't live up to their ideals.

- They may consider *Financial Security* or *Wealth* (gained the "right" way) to be an important part of their family ideals.

- They have strong ties to their area.

- They are very altruistic, as is their entire family.

ARCHETYPE LIKELIHOODS

These things are true for 75%–89% of the archetype:

- They are not interested in behaviors that display their values. They see their values like

Righteousness as deeply personal for themselves and their family members.

- They see social activities as a reward or to celebrate an accomplishment (e.g., children can play after their homework is done).

- They will work through important decisions carefully rather than making snap decisions.

- The patriarchy is alive and well within the family.

FUN FACTS

They appear only in two regions: China and the Middle East.

The country in the Middle East with the largest population of this archetype is Oman.

The only country in the Middle East where the Moral do not appear is Cyprus.

IN THEIR OWN WORDS:
Quotes from Survey Respondents

"There is a right way to do things, a way they should be done. It's not just one decision one time."

"The right way to behave is always the right way for my family."

"Acting in an honest way with consistent integrity is the best, solid foundation for family life."

"Different people have different interpretations of a good life, but only those with pure intentions are truly living a good life."

"I am not interested in products or services encouraging me to be someone I am not."

"My wife and I try to shelter our children from today's expectations for them to grow up fast and be adults while still teenagers."

"I expect honesty from everyone I engage with. The truth always comes out in the end."

"When deciding on a major purpose, I don't just consider what is best for my family now; I also consider the impact this purchase will have on them in the future."

CHAPTER 37

ARCHETYPE: THE CONNECTORS

GLOBAL RANKING: 13TH

Percentage of global population: 4%

Agreement on all 56 core human values: 78%

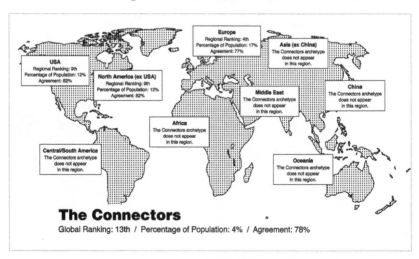

Europe
Regional Ranking: 4th
Percentage of Population: 17%
Agreement: 77%

Asia (ex China)
The Connectors archetype does not appear in this region.

USA
Regional Ranking: 9th
Percentage of Population: 12%
Agreement: 82%

North America (ex USA)
Regional Ranking: 9th
Percentage of Population: 12%
Agreement: 82%

China
The Connectors archetype does not appear in this region.

Middle East
The Connectors archetype does not appear in this region.

Africa
The Connectors archetype does not appear in this region.

Central/South America
The Connectors archetype does not appear in this region.

Oceania
The Connectors archetype does not appear in this region.

The Connectors
Global Ranking: 13th / Percentage of Population: 4% / Agreement: 78%

Where the Valuegraphics Archetype appears

274

This chart shows two things: the dominance of the archetype across the nine regions of the world and how often the people within the archetype agree with each other on the 56 core human values in the Valuegraphics Database.

WHAT MAKES THEM AN ARCHETYPE: The Unique Variable

These people view technology as a tool for *Belonging*. Technology is a means to an end.

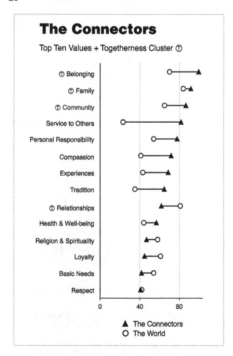

Archetype Valuegraphics Profile

From a possible 56 core human values, this chart compares the ranking of the top 10 values for the archetype to the same values for the population of the world. Also, since humans everywhere want to be with other humans, some of the five Togetherness Values will always appear. For definitions of the values, see Chapter 6.

ARCHETYPE CERTAINTIES

These things are true for at least 90% of the archetype:

- They are active social media users with multiple accounts that are likely to be linked.

- They are late adopters of new technology unless it improves their ability to connect with people.

- They are the ones who plan get-togethers in their social circles.

- They have wide-ranging and nonconservative political views.

- They have some traditional values.

- They have a deep family connection to their country—for example, fourth or fifth generation plus.

- They consider watching and participating in sports to be a social event.

ARCHETYPE LIKELIHOODS

These things are true for 75%–89% of the archetype:

- They will vote in elections but inconsistently.

- They are altruistic; they enjoy helping others.

- They are light users of technology for entertainment, if at all (e.g., won't have a Netflix subscription).
- They won't use technology for *Personal Growth* (e.g., online learning).

FUN FACTS

Only present in countries with majority-white populations.

The Connectors show up most in the United States, Italy, and France.

The archetype does not appear in Belgium or Russia.

IN THEIR OWN WORDS: Quotes from Survey Respondents

"I don't scroll Facebook; I just message the people I know."

"Technology is the greatest tool for healthy relationships, but it can also be the most harmful."

"I'm one of those people who still enjoys going into a real shop and interacting with real people."

"I prefer when people communicate with me using real words, not a bunch of pictures on a screen."

"I loathe shopping online; it's just not the same."

"I'm very loyal to brands and companies who treat me like an individual."

"If a business values me as a customer, that is something I don't forget."

CHAPTER 38

ARCHETYPE: THE SPIRITUAL

GLOBAL RANKING: 14TH

Percentage of global population: 4%

Agreement on all 56 core human values: 78%

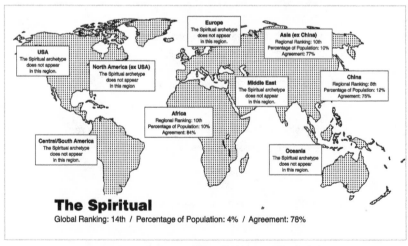

Where the Valuegraphics Archetype appears

This chart shows two things: the dominance of the archetype across the nine regions of the world and how often the people within the archetype agree with each other on the 56 core human values in the Valuegraphics Database.

WHAT MAKES THEM AN ARCHETYPE: The Unique Variable

Members of this archetype are religious or spiritual and practice their *Religion & Spirituality* with daily rituals. This archetype includes various forms of spiritual practice that fall outside what might be considered the mainstream religions: everything from a walk in the woods to the healing powers of crystals.

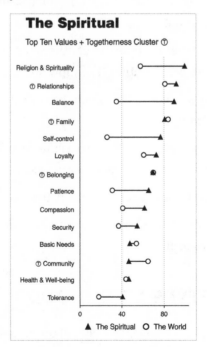

Archetype Valuegraphics Profile

From a possible 56 core human values, this chart compares the ranking of the top 10 values for the archetype to the same values for the population of the world. Also, since humans everywhere want to be with other humans, some of the five Togetherness Values will always appear. For definitions of the values, see Chapter 6.

ARCHETYPE CERTAINTIES

These things are true for at least 90% of the archetype:

- They live a balanced lifestyle (interestingly, few used "harmony" to describe this).

- They believe in moderation. They are unlikely to deprive themselves of anything but also unlikely to go without.

- They are very supportive of others but unlikely to have a word for this. It's simply how they live.

- They are somewhat political; they vote (in democratic countries).

- They are likely to cite their parents as an influence on their values and religious practice.

- They are the least likely of all groups to have children.

- They are extremely unlikely to have ever left their country of origin.

ARCHETYPE LIKELIHOODS

These things are true for 75%–89% of the archetype:

- They will share their spirituality/faith if asked but won't if unsolicited.

FUN FACTS

The largest appearances of the Spiritual are in Niger, Egypt, Nepal, and Thailand.

The archetype does not appear in Hong Kong or Albania.

In six regions of the world, the archetype is too insignificant to be counted. However, pockets of the archetype appear in some countries within those regions, specifically Brazil, Costa Rica, Italy, Greece, Croatia, and Malta.

IN THEIR OWN WORDS:
Quotes from Survey Respondents

"My religion gives my life meaning."

"I base my daily routine around my religious practice."

"A day without prayer is not a day at all."

"What I do wouldn't be considered religious by most, but my spiritual practices are important to me every day."

"If something is poor for my internal self, my external self won't buy it."

"I have a collection of knickknacks related to my spiritual side and can spend hours browsing in shops that sell these things."

"Experiences that feed and heal the natural energy last; other stuff doesn't."

"I consider religious practices to be a continuous fine-tuning that maintains balance. This is good for relationships, work, study, and the daily decisions we are forced to make."

CHAPTER 39

ARCHETYPE: THE OVERSPENT

GLOBAL RANKING: 15TH

Percentage of global population: 4%

Agreement on all 56 core human values: 76%

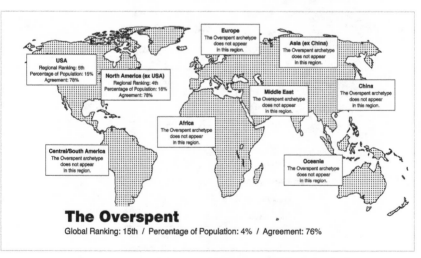

Europe
The Overspent archetype does not appear in this region.

Asia (ex China)
The Overspent archetype does not appear in this region.

USA
Regional Ranking: 5th
Percentage of Population: 15%
Agreement: 78%

North America (ex USA)
Regional Ranking: 4th
Percentage of Population: 18%
Agreement: 78%

China
The Overspent archetype does not appear in this region.

Middle East
The Overspent archetype does not appear in this region.

Africa
The Overspent archetype does not appear in this region.

Central/South America
The Overspent archetype does not appear in this region.

Oceania
The Overspent archetype does not appear in this region.

The Overspent

Global Ranking: 15th / Percentage of Population: 4% / Agreement: 76%

Where the Valuegraphics Archetype appears

This chart shows two things: the dominance of the archetype across the nine regions of the world and how often the people within the archetype agree with each other on the 56 core human values in the Valuegraphics Database.

WHAT MAKES THEM AN ARCHETYPE: The Unique Variable

The Overspent are living in debt that is at least double their income. It is important to note that this state of indebtedness does not discriminate; there are people in all economic strata represented here.

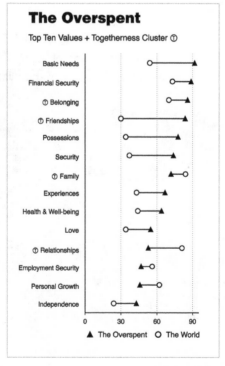

Archetype Valuegraphics Profile

From a possible 56 core human values, this chart compares the ranking of the top 10 values for the archetype to the same values for the population of the world. Also, since humans everywhere want to be with other humans, some of the five Togetherness Values will always appear. For definitions of the values, see Chapter 6.

ARCHETYPE CERTAINTIES

These things are true for at least 90% of the archetype:

- They are unlikely to have a formal education beyond high school.
- They are attracted to interactive entertainment, such as gaming.
- They have voted for multiple political parties.
- They are huge sports fans.
- They value *Friendships* as much or more than they value *Family*.

ARCHETYPE LIKELIHOODS

These things are true for 75%–89% of the archetype:

- They are likely to be users of some recreational drug.
- They play some sort of musical instrument.
- They are unattracted to financial services (e.g., financial planners, budgeting services, etc.).
- They are uninterested in politics even though they vote in each election they are eligible for.

FUN FACTS

The largest appearance of the Overspent overall is in the United States.

The largest appearance of the Overspent who are unconcerned about their debt is in Canada.

The largest appearance of the Overspent who find themselves in this situation because of factors beyond their control is in Jamaica.

This archetype does not appear in the Dominican Republic or Cuba.

This archetype appears in New Zealand, South Africa, and Malaysia even though their regions don't have this archetype overall.

IN THEIR OWN WORDS:
Quotes from Survey Respondents

"I've been in debt most of my adult life."

"We rely on credit most months and never get ahead."

"For me, life comes before any desire to be financially responsible."

"Our monthly income doesn't meet our monthly expenses."

"If I want something, I'll buy it even if I don't have the cash."

"I often buy similar things to what others have."

"My credit cards are my best friends, and our relationships will never die."

"I'm very influenced by the trends of the day."

"The kids get what they want. It just depends on the time of the month whether we have cash or if it goes on a card to worry about later."

"I'd prefer trying a new restaurant or going to a new place than worrying about my budget."

CHAPTER 40

CONCLUSION

ARE DEMOGRAPHICS REALLY DEAD?

AS A TOOL TO UNDERSTAND, ENGAGE, AND ACTIVATE people, they are. They are truly broken. They haven't worked for a very long time. Yet nearly every day, I stumble across another consultant peddling so-called knowledge about how to engage Generation Z in the workplace or some other such rubbish. And we keep hearing from clients about how they spent shocking amounts of money on demographic personas that clump customers and prospects into stereotypes based on age, income, gender, and the like. But what are you supposed to do with that? A segment of female baby boomers who make $200,000 a year means...what exactly? That you should make everything pink, avoid technology, and maybe scatter some luxury signals here and there so that it all feels upscale? Please.

And what else have we got? Psychographic data collection technologies keep evolving in ways that make my head spin. But they all track the same thing: history. If you can track something, it's because it has already happened. We are spending bajillions to drown ourselves in historical data. But if you want to know how to engage and activate people tomorrow, it's not enough to know what they did last week.

No one can predict the future, of course, but I hope in this book I've made at least this one point clear. The only way to see into the hearts and minds of human beings—and peer into the future of what they will do next—is to identify their core human values because our values drive everything we do. Everything.

Remember the story about the sturdy three-legged stool of audience insights?

1. The first leg is demographics, and we still need them in a limited way, to describe *what* people are because sometimes it matters.

2. The second leg is psychographics—all that data about what happened already. Because history can be a good teacher.

3. But unless we have valuegraphics as the third leg of the stool, we can't ever hope to know who people truly are and what they will do next.

The simple truth is that humans are neurologically,

psychologically, and sociologically hardwired to spend their lives in pursuit of what they value. We can't help ourselves; it's what being human is. And it's that shared humanity that prompted us to launch the Valuegraphics Project and create a replacement for broken demographic profiles. Now that it's complete, we have a kind of global encyclopedia of human behavior. We know why people do what they do and what will engage them next.

PEOPLE ARE EITHER BAKERS OR COOKS

Bakers love recipe books filled with photos of predetermined food-porn outcomes. If you set out to bake a pineapple upside-down cake and follow the directions precisely, you will get what you wanted.

Cooks are the anti-bakers. They know they want to make dinner for four people, but how they arrive at the destination depends on many variables. They will look at the ingredients they have on hand and maybe slip out to the store to see what looks fresh. They might need to chop some things, dice others, and blend a few things in the food processor. Ingredients might be broiled, roasted, fried, or steamed. They use intuition, experience, and experimentation to get to a satisfying result, with perhaps several course corrections required before they create a dish that makes the dinner a gastronomic success.

This book is for cooks. Bakers are not going to like it one bit. The answers that marketers and creators need today are not as simple as following a recipe for a Florentine tart. The answers we need are far more complex, involving intuitive choices between multiple techniques and ingredients. Most of all, valuegraphic answers require your own sociological imagination and industry experience—things that no cookbook can possibly provide. If you intend to use what I've written, it's best to think of this as a collaborative effort between you, me, and all the other stakeholders who will be standing around in the kitchen. Aren't those the best dinner parties, after all, where everyone has a glass of cabernet in one hand and gets involved in the process?

I promise it's worth the effort! Nothing beats the outcome of a good collab in the kitchen. And it's not as complicated as it might seem. Let's take one last look at the four steps I've laid out in the previous chapters.

1. **STEP ONE:** Send out the survey and tally the results. Use whatever means you have at your disposal to get this simple 15-question survey out there into the hands of the people you want to engage. This is like going to the grocery store and collecting the raw ingredients for the meal—a necessary step before you can start to create.

2. **STEP TWO:** Find your Superhero Archetype and any sidekicks, too. Once you've come home from the store with your primary ingredients, it's a good idea to read up on them and know what they are capable of doing. A baked ham is different from a roast goose, after all. That's all this step is about—diving a bit deeper into the specifics that are most vital to your success.

3. **STEP THREE:** Check the charts for your region. Oh good grief, the metaphor is wearing thin now, but bear with me. This step is like rummaging around in the pantry to see what else you can find that might be useful before you begin the process of creation. That box of breadcrumbs and tin of tomato paste might be the secret ingredients in the entrée your dinner guests will talk about for years to come.

4. **STEP FOUR:** Use the Values Thinking Process. It's finally time to create! You know by now more or less what you want to make, and this simple process will organize your thoughts to get you there.

Of course, if all of that seems too chaotic and you'd rather have a professional chef whip up a sumptuous feast, you can always hire us. This is the crux of what we do at the Valuegraphics Research Company. Organizations ask us to help them understand what makes their target audiences tick, and we deliver delicious results with enough statistical accuracy to earn you a PhD at the Ivy League school of your choosing.

NOW LET'S TACKLE SOMETHING EVEN BIGGER

So far, I've focused most of my energy in this book on one single idea: that values and valuegraphics are as much as eight times more effective.

But there's something even bigger here, something far

more important that we can accomplish together. In fact, the whole book has been leading up to this.

This is why we do what we do.

Demographics are divisive. We start every conversation in every boardroom about every new product or service or brand by defining a target audience. And it's always based on us versus them. Young versus old. Rich versus poor. Black versus white. Male versus female. No wonder the world around us is so full of strife when everything is born from such blatantly divisive thinking.

The longer we keep using these outdated demographic labels, the longer we perpetuate the demographic stereotypes fueling racism, sexism, ageism, homophobia, and the like. These social injustices are the direct result of continuing to view the world the way our ancestors did.

Thankfully, the world is waking up to the power and potential of a values-driven view of humanity. If we simply discard the harmful and hurtful demographic stereotypes from days gone by, we can be more effective at work and build a better world, too. We can do well while we do good.

It's not hard. If we just change the way we look at the world, we can change the world.

THIS BOOK MARKS A MOMENT IN TIME. IT'S A RECORD OF what I've learned so far and includes some tools you can use to put this knowledge to use, including a five-minute video synopsis of this book you can watch anytime at **www.valuegraphicsbook.com**.

But this isn't over. Far from it. It's only the beginning. And it will never end.

Convincing everyone in the world to embrace a new way to understand each other will be an uphill journey for the rest of my life. And others who come after me will need to keep climbing the mountain because we will never reach the top. There is no top. There's no end to what we can learn about our shared human values and the role they can play in making the world a better place.

So I'll keep sharing what I learn. Please follow me on LinkedIn for updates. And read the results of new studies as we release them at www.valuegraphics.com. We have an aggressive research publishing schedule and love talking about what we find.

And would you please do the same? Would you share your thoughts, your ideas, and the results you see from using valuegraphics in your work? Maybe you'd like to share the five-minute video synopsis mentioned above. If you are done with your copy of this book, perhaps you could pass it along to someone else. The more people talking about the enormous magnetic power and game-changing potential of shared human values, the better.

CASE STORIES

DEAR RENTAL MANAGER: ONE PROPERTIES GETS MAIL

ONE PROPERTIES, A REAL ESTATE DEVELOPMENT AND property management company, was experiencing tremendous growth in its property management business.

In March 2020, as COVID-19 began to rapidly spread around the world, the company wanted to boost tenant retention rates to reduce costly turnover. They had a critical question about their strategy:

"What do apartment renters care about today?"

ONE Properties commissioned a Valuegraphics Profile of their target audience to look past the traditional demographics of age and income. From the 56 values that are the source code for every human behavior and emotion, several audience segments emerged. In particular, these four values sparked intense internal discussion:

- Relationships
- Belonging
- Personal Growth
- Experiences

Renters highly value *Relationships*, far more than the general population. They are driven toward anything that will create real connections with the people in their orbit.

Similarly important, *Belonging* is a major hot button. They want to fit in; they want to feel "These are my people!"

Understanding the importance of *Personal Growth*, which you might define as a constant desire to "be a better me" every day, led to amenity and in-suite FF&E strategies designed to deliver, as did the high value placed on new and interesting *Experiences.*

These four fundamental results became the magnetic North Star values and guided the ONE Properties team as they created a new approach. They developed policies and processes on how best to engage and support residents by embedding those values in the DNA of the business.

The company adopted a hotel-style customer service model, enabled employees with the mandate to follow through on maintenance and operations issues raised by tenants, invested in tenant-focused roles like the Resident Experience Manager, and launched a robust social program.

Each decision in planning and operations was values-driven and based on valuegraphic data.

ONE Properties first rolled out its new platform at a 444-unit residential building catering to urban professionals in March 2020, when the city was stressed not only by COVID-19 but also a steady stream of negative employment and economic indicators.

Within a few months, despite the global health crisis, tenant satisfaction went up, lease renewals improved, and vacancies were reduced.

And there was an unexpected outcome, too.

Company management started to receive unsolicited letters of gratitude from building residents who were happy with ONE Properties' personal touch, responsiveness, compassion, social focus, and the building assets and amenities. Tenants were writing thank-you notes to their building management company.

"It is extremely difficult to please everyone in a large apartment building, but you are doing a great job."

"The staff truly make us feel they care about us and want to make our time living here a great one!"

"I've been living in the building now for three years and just signed another year's lease. With customer service like this, I'll certainly be a long-term tenant."

By informing decision-making with what residents value—what they care about most—ONE Properties forged a path to strong business growth.

"We are working to be an industry leader," says Courtney Dulai, who is leading the multifamily resident experience at ONE Properties. "If we continue to follow the North Star values, we will get there."

ONLINE SHOPPING AND THE TREASURE HUNTERS

For a keynote speech I gave to online retailers, we profiled shoppers who buy something online at least once a week. The data from the Valuegraphics Profile revealed four target audience segments.

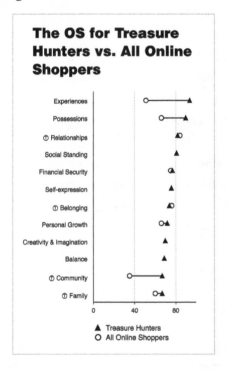

The OS for Treasure Hunters vs. All Online Shoppers

▲ Treasure Hunters
O All Online Shoppers

Three of those segments seem obvious: people who like to avoid crowds, those who find online shopping convenient, or those who can't find what they want near where they live. But it's the fourth segment, which makes up 20% of the online shopping universe, that I want to talk about here.

I call this group the Treasure Hunters because they are as interested in the hunt as they are in whatever they are hunting for. The process of researching, discovering, comparing, considering, and securing a product or service is an experience they savor and enjoy. It's both the journey and the destination for these digital experience acquisitors. The chart shows how their Valuegraphics Profile is different from the other segments in the study.

How these values can help you with your online sales will depend entirely on what you are trying to sell. But across all categories, these customers will be drawn to your offering if you can give them the thrill of the hunt they are looking for. Only you know how to do that best, but here are some off-the-cuff ideas.

The value these shoppers place on *Possessions* isn't surprising to see because after all, this is a group defined by their desire to hunt for things. But look at the massive 24% difference in the impact that *Possessions* has on the behavior of this segment compared to the overall online shopping population. It's hugely and uniquely magnetic, this value. How can you make what you sell into a precious and treasured possession?

- They will appreciate beautiful packaging. Can your packaging be reused for other things or perhaps for storage of whatever they've purchased from you?

- They will devour stories about the makers of whatever you are selling, where the materials were sourced, and how long it took to make. Nothing makes a possession more of a possession than layers and layers of story. Can you include stories in the package? Can you reference these narratives in your online store? Social media seems like an obvious place to double down on the stories behind your products, too.

Even more fascinating is how they would respond if you could find a way to let them flex their *Creativity* and *Self-Expression* muscles. How can you involve them in the creation process? Are there opportunities for personalization and customization in what you do? Can you tie this to the *Social Standing* boost that they are looking for?

"Julia, where on earth did you find that beautiful painting hanging over your fireplace?"

"It took forever, but I tracked it down through an obscure artists-run-cooperative gallery space in a suburb of Antwerp. There was a hellishly byzantine process to secure shipping permits to bring it out of the EU, but I found a way to subvert most of the rigamarole and get it done. When it arrived, I opened the crate and plopped it up there and haven't given it much thought ever since. But it is nice, isn't it? How is your martini?"

Here's another random thought: you might want to consider making your site feel like a rare discovery, something that only a select few treasure hunters have found. I'm thinking about a legendary cocktail bar in New York City that you had to access through a phone booth in the back of a greasy-spoon diner. The only way you knew it was there was if someone told you. It was a secret. And it was uproariously successful as a result.

THE ENVIRONMENTAL DEFENSE FUND AND THE GUILTY AS CHARGED

For more than 50 years, the Environmental Defense Fund (EDF) has been one of the world's leading environmental organizations. They are based in Washington, DC, and support a wide range of environmental issues around the globe. They take on climate change and other grave environmental threats using a variety of tools and techniques.

To help guide fundraising strategies, we profiled their donors who intended to keep giving. We found some audience segments that we see time and again whenever we are profiling target audiences in the environmental space.

For example, we saw a group we call the Personal Environmentalists, who see environmental issues with a mirror: they are most motivated by how environmental issues affect them and the ones they love. We also saw another group of familiar friends, the Collective Hero Environmentalists. They want to band together with like-minded folks, put on their superhero capes, and go save the world together as one big slogan-chanting group. And there was yet another segment who will—to the point of being workaholics—do everything they can to ensure a good life for their family. This third group supports EDF because they want their family to have a clean and safe world to live in for generations to come.

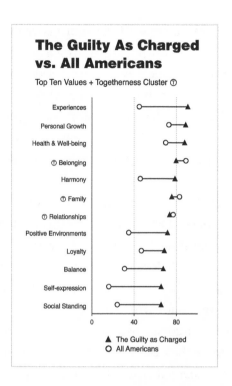

The Guilty As Charged vs. All Americans

Top Ten Values + Togetherness Cluster ⓣ

Experiences	
Personal Growth	
Health & Well-being	
ⓣ Belonging	
Harmony	
ⓣ Family	
ⓣ Relationships	
Positive Environments	
Loyalty	
Balance	
Self-expression	
Social Standing	

Scale: 0 — 40 — 80

▲ The Guilty as Charged
O All Americans

There are specific Valuegraphics Profiles for each of those three segments and all sorts of other insights, but let's focus on a fascinating fourth segment we have never seen before. I call them the Guilty as Charged.

The Guilty as Charged are people who highly value *Experiences*. You can see from the chart how much more importance they place on this value compared to the rest of the American population. But this particular kind of experience junkie is also hyper-aware of their carbon footprint. They donate to EDF to assuage their guilt.

They know that flying all over the place for their adventures increases their own personal impact on the health of the planet. So they donate to make themselves feel better.

Their donations are frequent but irregular because they travel frequently and irregularly. The size of their donations varies based on how damaging they consider a particular trip to be.

A hush fell over the boardroom when I shared this Valuegraphics Profile for the first time. One person summed up how others were feeling when she said, "If these people know what they are doing is bad for the planet, they should stop doing it."

I love the memory of that moment for two reasons.

First, it made it abundantly clear that these people in the boardroom at the EDF were there, working as hard as they did, because their values were in alignment with their work. It's always inspiring to meet people who are doing what they are supposed to be doing.

Second, it's a great illustration of the power of our core values. Despite their concern for the environment, asking the Guilty as Charged to put aside the value of *Experiences* would be like asking them to stop breathing. They'd rather part with their hard-earned money than be out of alignment with the things they care about most.

So if you were the EDF, what would you do with this information? How would you design a fundraising strategy to connect the dots between the organization and what these people care about? I'm not going to tell you what the EDF did, as that's their business, but here are a couple of ideas that would earn an A+ in Values Thinking if it were up to me to decide.

If we focus on the value these people place on *Experiences*, without even looking at the rest of their valuegraphics, there's an obvious play to be made. Offer them alternative *Experiences* that have a net-zero or even a net-positive effect on the planet.

Can you arrange for these donors, in exchange for a donation of a suitable size, to be part of an environmental research project? Maybe they could be field workers and help scientists collect samples or readings. Maybe they need to still fly to these adventures, but if their energies are focused on activities that will help Mother Earth, perhaps that's a better end result.

And since these folks are already hyper-aware of the direct connection between their actions and their carbon footprint, are there other ways to connect these same dots? Could other things that they do trigger donations, too?

For example, what if you leverage the importance they place on *Personal Growth* and make it easy to feel like better consumers every time they shop? What if they could donate a token amount every time they bought a grocery item packaged in an environmentally unfriendly way? Could an app be developed to scan grocery barcodes and calculate a dollar amount that is automatically transferred to the EDF with a single click? Even better, could you strike a deal with a large grocery chain to offer this option at every checkout? Then all you'd need to do is reach out to the Guilty as Charged and suggest they start shopping in those stores. What grocery chain would say no to that?

BRUNELLO CUCINELLI IN CHINA AND THE UNITED STATES

Writing a book is a lot of hard work, so it's perfectly acceptable to indulge myself from time to time, don't you think?

And if that authorial self-indulgence results in an excellent story to add to the book, then so much the better, am I right? I sure hope you agree because this case story means a lot to me. It's about one of my favorite brands in the world, Brunello Cucinelli. If you are reading this, Mr. Cucinelli, what follows is a tip of my hat to you.

For those of you who aren't familiar with the outrageously beautiful and well-made clothing and accessories that Brunello Cucinelli is known for, I'm not sure what else to say except they are outrageously beautiful and well made. And yes, reassuringly expensive. But there's a reason. You are not simply buying clothes; you are buying into an experiment in brand building based on values.

Mr. Cucinelli has been slowly reinvigorating small-town life in northern Italy in places with a history of making beautiful clothes. The old factory looms and mills are running again; the nonnas are bringing lunch to the workers; the churches and schools are full once more; and the kids are learning the trades once perilously close to being lost.[25] In short, the brand is based on pursuing a set of values. If I were to guess, I'd say the values that the Cucinelli brand has chosen to pursue include *Community*, *Harmony*, *Respect*, *Tradition*, *Patience*, and most definitely *Service to Others*. Even though there are probably faster ways to scale and smarter ways to grow than by rebuilding the past, giving people pride, and creating a future for the families of your employees, this example of doing well by doing good seems to be working out fine.

But how do the values of Cucinelli customers compare?

---

25 To learn more about Mr. Cucinelli, visit https://www.brunellocucinelli.com/en/my-life.html

Are the brand values aligned with their customers' values? Does it vary from one market to the next? Is there a difference between current Cucinelli customers and the prospective customers who will fuel future growth?

We surveyed a statistically representative sample of 1,850 people who consider themselves regular purchasers, as well as another 1,850 people who are Cucinelli fans but, for one reason or another, have not yet committed to buying their first piece.

And since this custom Valuegraphics Profile was at least partly for my own pleasure, I thought it would be interesting to do the same thing in another part of the world. So in addition to the United States, we did the whole thing all over again in China.

I could fill a few pages with demographics and psychographics specific to each country and the audience segments we discovered. But unless you are the director of marketing for the Cucinelli brand, these details will not be that exciting. So let's stick to the most fun bits, starting with these three general observations that I found quite intriguing:

- The Chinese are more likely to feel that wearing Cucinelli will benefit their family. They see it as a means to an end. If you look successful, their thinking goes, it will help you be successful, and ultimately your family will benefit.

- On the other hand, the US buyer considers Cucinelli (and other luxury purchases) as an end goal, not as a tool to accomplish something else. In fact, we saw this same distinction between the

Chinese and US target audiences for one of our clients, another luxury clothing brand we had profiled before. And although we have only these two brands to consider, it makes me wonder if the same thing is true across the entire high-end clothing category. In China, it seems, what you wear is a tool to help you get where you want to be. In the United States, however, luxury clothing is enjoyed for its own sake.

- People in the United States frame their attraction to Cucinelli brand values in terms of respect. In other words, "I respect what they stand for. Good for them." Whereas in China, people emulate the brand, as in, "I want to be like that, too. It will be good for me."

Cucinelli Customers in the United States versus China

Different values drive Cucinelli customers in the United States and China, so brand messages will be more potent if they are tweaked slightly to reflect what people care about in each part of the world. It's not that entirely different positioning is required, but there is an opportunity to heighten the magnetic appeal of the brand for each market.

It's like two groups of ice-cream fanatics: one group loves chocolate, and the other prefers butter pecan. Both groups love ice cream and would probably eat any flavor.

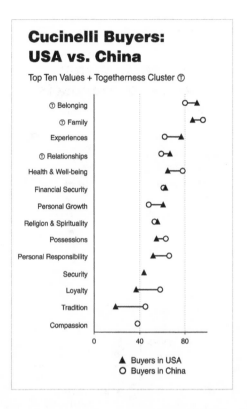

**Cucinelli Buyers:
USA vs. China**

Top Ten Values + Togetherness Cluster ⓣ

ⓣ Belonging	
ⓣ Family	
Experiences	
ⓣ Relationships	
Health & Well-being	
Financial Security	
Personal Growth	
Religion & Spirituality	
Possessions	
Personal Responsibility	
Security	
Loyalty	
Tradition	
Compassion	

0   40   80

▲ Buyers in USA
O Buyers in China

But if you know the exact flavor they crave, why not make both groups swoon with as much personalization as you can muster? In other words, why water down the results you could achieve in both regions simply for the sake of a uniform campaign?

Of course, you might find a way to blend both Valuegraphics Profiles without diminishing the appeal in either market, much as you might build an ice cream sundae with scoops of both chocolate and butter pecan. But there's a risk. If you don't get the flavor proportions right, you'll end up with a confusing mess that doesn't appeal to anyone.

Cucinelli Customers versus Prospects

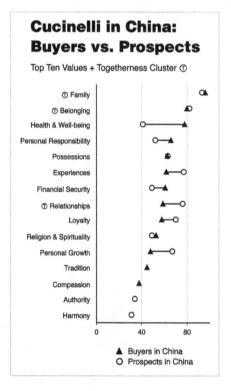

**Cucinelli in China:
Buyers vs. Prospects**

Top Ten Values + Togetherness Cluster ⑦

There is a big difference between customers and prospects in China, while the differences seem to be less dramatic in the United States. Even a quick glance shows how the comparative data lines up in a more uniform way on the United States chart than on the chart for China.

Tactically, it's impossible to create a different brand position for current versus future customers in the same geographic market. You need to find a happy middle ground that works for both groups. Consequently, in China, the challenge is to embrace a wider variety of people with a platform that reflects more disparate values.

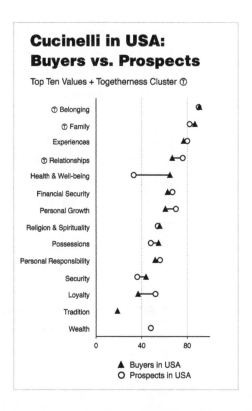

Cucinelli in USA:
Buyers vs. Prospects

Top Ten Values + Togetherness Cluster ⓣ

- ⓣ Belonging
- ⓣ Family
- Experiences
- ⓣ Relationships
- Health & Well-being
- Financial Security
- Personal Growth
- Religion & Spirituality
- Possessions
- Personal Responsibility
- Security
- Loyalty
- Tradition
- Wealth

0   40   80

▲ Buyers in USA
O Prospects in USA

Here's an example. Customers in China are influenced far more by *Health & Well-Being* than prospects are. Prospects, however, are huge on *Experiences.*

To illustrate how values can drive solutions, let's pretend the assignment is to plan an event in the Chinese market. The objective of this event is to reward your best customers and jump-start sales for a new season. While we're at it, let's see if we can also convert some prospects into customers. And since we're pretending, I've decided to pretend the budget for this event is limitless.

What if you staged an elaborate outdoor dinner in an extraordinary location that connects the brand to the value of

Health & Well-Being. Guests are seated at a long, linen-draped table, centerfield in a football stadium that you've rented for the occasion. Transportation to and from the dinner is part of the show, of course. Cucinelli-clad models with luscious Italian accents who are (magically) also fluent in Chinese will chauffeur guests to the dinner in luxury sedans.

You invite your very best customers, of course. But interspersed around the table, you place prospects who are likely candidates for conversion to loyal customers. Why? Because the importance they place on *Experiences* will leave them feeling like they have scored a sartorial goal by being part of this special event. If this doesn't convert them, nothing will!

And since this pretending game is so much fun, let's go crazy. There's a fashion show during the cocktail hour with famous football players sporting the latest collection. Look! Here comes David Beckham wearing the new indigo-dyed cashmere dinner jacket!

And of course, we will send everyone home with a gift. It's a butter-soft leather soccer ball created by Cucinelli artisans specifically for this night, autographed by all the football stars and by Mr. Cucinelli, too.

Let's dissect this fantasy event using the values on the chart for Chinese customers and prospects. We did a great job using *Health & Well-Being* and *Experiences*. But I'd argue that strategic storytelling around this event, combined with a thoughtful lead-up and follow-through, would also activate the values of *Belonging*, *Relationships*, and *Possessions*, too.

"Now, wait a minute," I hear you saying, jabbing your

finger at me to emphasize your point. "Who wouldn't enjoy going to that event?" It's a great question. And you are not wrong. It sounds like nearly anyone would have a good time.

But this event originated in the data. It was easy to dream up an evening of mythical proportions because we had a magnetic North Star. We knew what this crowd of luxury shoppers would react to. See the difference? *Our dinner was conceived because we had the data to support this particular idea instead of a gut-level hunch.*

Let's shift our focus to the United States.

Have a look at the chart for American customers and prospects, and you'll notice that with a few exceptions, their values align.[26] It's far easier to think about both customers and prospects in America as one big, happy, commingled target audience. We see common ground on values like *Experiences*, *Personal Responsibility*, and *Financial Security*, for example. What could we do with only those three values to appeal to current buyers and prospects alike?

Let's pretend we've been tasked with reworking the US version of the company website, and our goal today is to establish the key communication goals. What do we want our American target audience to learn about the brand?

If *Experiences*, *Personal Responsibility*, and *Financial Security* are the unifying values we want to activate, it would be easy to support a messaging strategy like the following:

- Emphasize the timelessness and durability of the clothing, and remind website visitors how these investment garments will last a lifetime. Owning

---

26   There's still a big disconnect on the importance of *Health & Well-Being* as there was in China. I wonder if it also exists in other parts of the world? It would be fascinating to find out.

clothes that are timeless and enduring is a financially smart thing to do, which appeals to those who value *Financial Security.*

- The decision to acquire high-quality, durable clothing is the opposite of disposable-fashion consumption, which means the buyer is taking *Personal Responsibility* for walking on the planet with a lighter footprint.

- Traditional techniques and tools in the factories contribute significantly to the well-deserved reputation for quality craftsmanship, like the complicated and oh-so-elegant Neapolitan shoulder, a trademark of Cucinelli tailoring that stretches back hundreds of years. What an *Experience* it is to wear clothing with this kind of heritage artistry sewn right in!

Cucinelli's marketing team is no stranger to these storylines, of course. That's why Cucinelli customers and prospects are attracted to the brand in the first place: because these values are already present. Remember, what we value determines everything we do, including our brand preferences.

However, with values statistically identified and extrapolated from a dataset of more than three-quarters of a million surveys, it's now clear to the Cucinelli marketing team how important these particular values are compared to all others. They can spend more time connecting the dots between what they've got and what their target audience cares about most of all.

Cucinelli's Influenced Loyalists

Every time we analyze the data for a target audience, several audience segments appear. It's like looking at any collection of things and organizing them into groups.

Think of a table covered with cards and letters you've received from friends and family over the years. You could organize them into piles based on who sent them to you. Or you could arrange them based on the year they were written. Or the color of the ink used to write them.

Some segments show up quite frequently in the work we do for various clients in various sectors of the economy. But we found a rare one in the data for Cucinelli prospects. This is a group of people who are a group because of one simple thing: they want to be loyal to the same things as their heroes and mentors. We call these people the Influenced Loyalists.

The Influenced Loyalists may follow the work of a business guru who wears Cucinelli. Or perhaps they are fans of a famous Cucinelli-clothed singer, writer, or actor who has had a huge impact on their life. Maybe it's a family member they admire who wears the brand. Someone influential in their life wears the brand, and that makes them want to do the same. Convincing this group to buy the brand is about, at least in part, making sure they know who else is wearing the brand. And given that this segment represents 17% of the Cucinelli prospect audience, activating their values could significantly boost sales.

To see how different they are from the rest of the Cucinelli audience, have a look at the chart. The differences

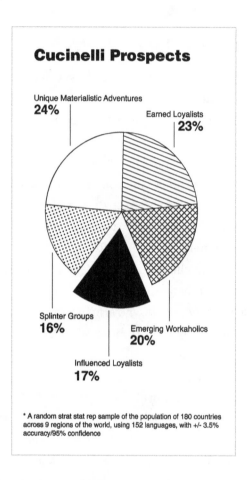

Cucinelli Prospects

Unique Materialistic Adventures
24%

Earned Loyalists
23%

Splinter Groups
16%

Emerging Workaholics
20%

Influenced Loyalists
17%

* A random strat stat rep sample of the population of 180 countries across 9 regions of the world, using 152 languages, with +/- 3.5% accuracy/95% confidence

are a gift in this scenario because those disparities make it easy to engage these prospects in a precise way.

Let's assume we have been assigned a broad marketing challenge: the CEO has asked us to boost engagement with the Influenced Loyalists. We've looked at the data and decided to focus on the values of *Loyalty*, *Relationships*, and *Personal Responsibility*, as these are three uniquely dominant values for this segment.

We know our target audience is influenced by individuals

toward whom they feel a sense of loyalty. So one obvious way to engage them would be to find a brand ambassador who inspires that loyalty. Here are some guiding principles we could use to help us make a selection:

- It would need to be someone who is borderless, who appeals to prospects regardless of where they live, and who has a story that shows how *Loyalty* reaps dividends.

- Furthermore, because these prospects value *Relationships*, this brand ambassador should feel friendly and approachable.

- And finally, it should be someone who is doing good things in the world, someone who has taken on some *Personal Responsibility* to make things better for people.

If the company could find a brand ambassador who meets those qualifications, this segment of the Cucinelli audience would be hard-pressed to look away. And at the risk of sounding sycophantic, I wonder if it might not be Brunello Cucinelli himself. Often, when a brand pushes the founder to the front of the room, it is because of the founder's ego. But in this case, the data fully supports the decision.

Brunello Cucinelli is a globally known figure, already prominent within the brand's communication strategy. He is a leader who comes across as personable and approachable. He has spent a good portion of his life reviving a small town and giving the inhabitants a better life. If that's not *Loyalty* on parade, loyalty to a set of values shared by this segment of the target audience, I'm not sure what is.

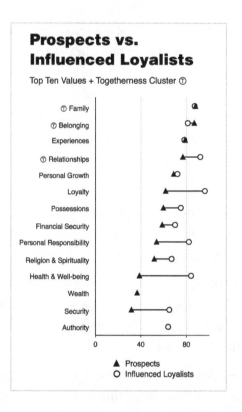

Prospects vs. Influenced Loyalists

Top Ten Values + Togetherness Cluster ⓣ

Cucinelli, the company, could do worse than to increase the visibility of Brunello Cucinelli significantly and push him to the front in more ways than they do at present. The Influenced Loyalists would reward this approach in tangible ways.

THE APPLE LINEUPPERS

Apple is one of the most successful and beloved brands in the world, so it might seem a bit cheeky of me to offer suggestions. What could valuegraphics bring to one of the most sophisticated marketing machines on the planet? But I like being cheeky. So here we go.

What we know about Apple customers comes from the three-quarters of a million-plus surveys we conducted around the world to build our benchmark database. A lot of people used Apple as an example when we asked them to name their favorite brands.

In other words, enough people voluntarily talked about Apple when they were telling us about their values, wants, needs, and expectations that we are able to see patterns in the noise. Of course, if Apple wanted a full Valuegraphics Profile for their target audience, what we'd find would be far more robust than this. What follows is like those little samples handed out in the grocery store by people wearing chef's jackets. It's only a taste test, but it's an intriguing mouthful.

We saw a group of people in the data who had an adventurous streak and valued *Experiences* more than most people do. We call this group of Apple fans the Lineuppers and here's why.

These folks especially like experiences that result in materialistic things. And they have a preference for experiences that repeat. Once they find an adventure they like, they want it to happen again and again. We call them *repeat materialistic adventurers.*

For example, standing in line for the new iPhone release is an adventure with a materialistic outcome, and lining up every single time there is a new iPhone release means it's a materialistic adventure that repeats.

Curiously, Apple Lineuppers are markedly different from other materialistic repeat adventurers we've encountered (in various product categories) because the value they place on *Personal Growth* is quite low when compared to

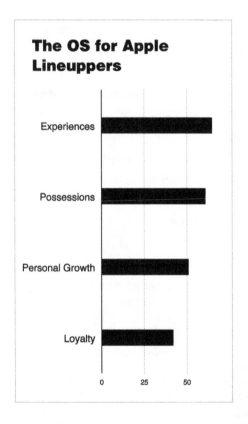

The OS for Apple Lineuppers

Experiences	
Possessions	
Personal Growth	
Loyalty	

0   25   50

the general population. Apple products are not tools to help them make better things or think bigger thoughts or grow in a personal or professional way. Or, better put, *Personal Growth* is not the primary driver behind the behavior of this customer group.

In fact, their *Loyalty* to Apple is the result of an incredibly sophisticated UX that aligns with the importance they place on *Experiences* and *Possessions*. They can't help but be drawn to a possession that is an experience and an experience that results in a possession. It's pure gold for these folks. Everything about visiting the Apple

Store delivers on these values. Consider the much-written-about efforts that Apple goes through to ensure that the normally mundane act of opening a box is transformed into a semi-spiritual ritual.

My advice to Apple is to do everything they possibly can to make their product feel like a treasured possession and find every opportunity to make all touchpoints feel like exciting experiences. I hope someone at Apple is taking notes because, well...never mind. Clearly Apple knows about these people and they have nailed it.

But still, it's nice to see that efforts to craft a repeat materialistic adventure for people who are loyal to anything that offers them a possession wrapped in an experience are, in fact, attracting exactly those people.

Last, *this is only one segment* of the Apple customer base. But sometimes it seems like this is the *only* segment Apple fixates on. I wonder what a custom Valuegraphics Profile might reveal about the remaining segments of the target audience who have made Apple such a success.

FIVE STAR SCHOOL SUPPLIES

ACCO Brands Corporation is one of the largest and most successful producers of academic, consumer, and business goods in the world.

ACCO's premium school supplies brands, like Five Star, do 75% of their annual back-to-school business in August alone—in an increasingly competitive market. It's a sector that requires constant innovation and a commitment to continuously learning more about their customers. That's why ACCO commissioned a Valuegraphics Profile to expand what they know about school-supply shoppers.

We delivered ACCO's custom study in January 2020 as the onset of COVID-19's global pandemic rattled business plans across the world. The timing was great, as the insights we presented showed various internal teams what their customers cared about most.

- The Valuegraphics Profile confirmed that the existing brand position matched what existing customers cared about. That certainty made forward planning less risky because everyone was confident that the brand stood on solid ground.

- Valuegraphic insights allowed marketing teams to think about engaging new customers in new ways and removed much of the risk from trying new messaging and themes.

- Engineering and product development departments used Values Thinking to inform new ideas for future product upgrades and innovations.

- Perhaps most notably, valuegraphic data helped uncover new ways to differentiate the brand against the competition.

Other brands continuously copy what ACCO gets up to—it's one of the burdens of being the best in the game. But with valuegraphic data, ACCO has proprietary, actionable insights on their customers and their marketplace that moves the needle in ways that the competition can't predict.

ESG AND THE NEXT GENERATION OF WEALTH

Trillions of dollars will change hands as the baby boomers pass along their wealth to the next generation, putting the children of the world's wealthiest people in control of significant fortunes.

This new generation of high net worth individuals—a group we call *The Inheritors*—will have different valuegraphics than their parents, which means anyone interested in reaching this desirable target audience must learn to adapt.

Misconceptions abound about how to connect with The Inheritors. For example, there's a belief that they will all be focused on doing good things while they make their money. But our data shows that only 20% of The Inheritors feel this way. And even though some people may be disappointed in this finding, the glass-half-full side of the argument is that 20% of the wealthiest people will be focused on doing well and doing good. That's nothing to sneeze at!

The Valuegraphics Profile of The Inheritors revealed a number of segments. As the name for this particular valuegraphic segment implies, these Inheritors are focused on environmental, social, and governance (ESG) considerations when it comes to investing. Correspondingly, they are also interested in what we might call ESG philanthropy.

I was initially surprised that *Environmentalism* did not show up as a top value. However, remember that we do not force our definitions of the 56 values on survey respondents. Instead, we measure where they are magnetically drawn on

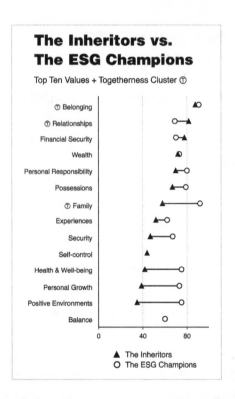

The Inheritors vs. The ESG Champions

Top Ten Values + Togetherness Cluster ⓣ

- ⓣ Belonging
- ⓣ Relationships
- Financial Security
- Wealth
- Personal Responsibility
- Possessions
- ⓣ Family
- Experiences
- Security
- Self-control
- Health & Well-being
- Personal Growth
- Positive Environments
- Balance

0 40 80

▲ The Inheritors
○ The ESG Champions

their own. And for this group, *Positive Environments* is a value that could encompass their environmentalist leanings.

People who value *Positive Environments* are engaged by anything that impacts their physical, mental, spiritual, or social environments in positive ways. They will be concerned about the environment as it relates to them personally and the people they love most. This means they will care deeply about their local forest being cut down, but when it comes to more abstract and far-flung environmental concerns, their engagement may be less direct.

There are other values they share in abundance, but let's take a closer look at just two: *Personal Responsibility* and *Possessions.*

Personal Responsibility is a value shared by people who want to make an impact by doing things themselves. They are the opposite of people who sit on the couch, watch the news, and say things like, "Somebody should do something about that." They are the ones who get up off the couch and go do whatever needs doing.

And I'm glad to see that *Possessions* shows in this Valuegraphics Profile. It makes them feel more human somehow, doesn't it? Despite their big hearts and their drive to do good things with their money, they still like their stuff! Lots more stuff than the other Inheritors, as it turns out.

How to Engage the ESG Champions

Let's say your environmental organization is launching a shoreline cleanup initiative. For the ESG Champions, it would be wise to ask them to personally come and participate in the cleanup instead of asking them to write a check.

Why? Because they will be magnetically drawn to the *Personal Responsibility* that picking up beach garbage delivers. What's more, if you stage the event on a Sunday when the kids are out of school, they'd be thrilled because it delivers on *Family*. An opportunity like this will be far more attractive for this target audience than the stereotypical not-for-profit black-tie gala fundraising dinner could ever be.

What else could you do to connect the dots between your event and the values these folks care about most?

Because of the value these people place on *Possessions*, could you send everyone home with a meaningful gift? How about something practical and reusable made of recycled ocean plastics—a net bag for shopping to replace disposable plastic bags at the grocery store?

And why not invite environmental scientists to participate, too, and chat about the positive steps your organization is taking to increase science-based stewardship of our oceans. Be sure to brief those scientists in advance so they stay focused on the *positive* changes that have been made possible through donor support. Remember, this target audience is driven by the value of *Positive Environments* and will turn off if the message is all doom and despair. After all, we must have hope for a better future because the alternative is unthinkable, and you don't need to be an ESG champion to see the logic in that.

VODKA VERSUS GIN: THE GREAT MARTINI DEBATE

If you've ever been to a party where martinis are on the menu, you may have overheard the good-natured arguments that inevitably ensue about what makes a better martini. Both sides of the debate have a firm belief that they are correct.

Gin drinkers generally argue that theirs is the original version and therefore the correct one. Vodka drinkers, although sometimes willing to concede the point about the origin of the cocktail, see no reason to be hidebound to tradition. After all, there was a time when handwritten letters were sent on horseback via the Pony Express, and that doesn't mean we should still be doing things that way.

I'm always curious about serious matters like this. And

since what we value determines what we do, there must be some difference in the valuegraphics of those who choose one kind of martini over the other. Here's a quick review of what a Valuegraphics Profile revealed.

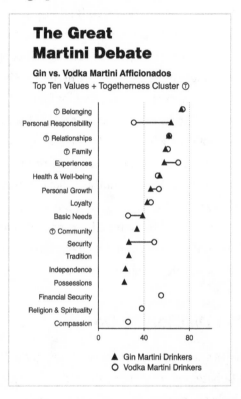

Team Gin is united around a set of core values that include *Personal Responsibility*, *Community*, and *Tradition*. I'm starting to see a persona here, someone who closely resembles the stereotype of a conservative gin martini drinker. They believe people should look after themselves and be upstanding members of the community, and they would never be caught dead with a martini that tastes like cranberries or green apples. They are likely suspicious of stuffed olives, and lemon twists are as much fruit as they can put up with. I'm imagining bowties, or at least a passing acquaintance with someone who wears one, and they see nothing odd about that.

On the other hand, Team Vodka is uninterested in *Community*, whereas *Relationships* are near the top of their chart. They much prefer spending time with people they already know. More unusual values are here, too. We don't see *Religion & Spirituality* show up in profiles for most products or services, and it's interesting that it did not show up for Team Gin—not even a little bit. *Compassion* is also a somewhat rare value, especially for a consumer profile like this.

If you also take into account the importance they place on *Security*, *Financial Security*, and *Basic Needs*, I could argue that compared to Team Gin, these folks are more worried about the future, and they have a strong tendency to care for those who are closest to them.

What's a Distillery to Do?

I could write a small book on what we know about the Great Martini Debate now that we've done this study. For both teams, there are several segments that appear, each with a unique Valuegraphics Profile. And if we did a deep dive to the level of specific brands, we could determine what attracts some people to Bombay Sapphire gin instead of Hendrick's, Beefeater, or Tanqueray.

But with the broadest of all possible brushstrokes, here's some high-level advice.

If I was a gin maker, I'd focus my marketing strategies

on teaching my customers how to be a master martini mix-
ologist. Why? Because it's a badge of honor, a tasty way to
reward yourself for getting things done, and it signals your
inclusion in a community of those in the know.

And if my gig was all about selling vodka? I'd focus my
communications and branding on building better bonds and
having fun. Because in these uncertain times we live in, you can
always count on your friends, and they can always count on you.

THE UNITED NATIONS FOUNDATION NOTHING BUT NETS CAMPAIGN

I just ended a Zoom meeting with an incredibly dedicated
team from the United Nations Foundation. How much fun
is it to write that sentence?

We were talking about raising funds for mosquito nets
in countries where a malaria-infected bug bite is still a death
sentence. Every two minutes, a child dies from malaria—a
deadly yet preventable disease. The Nothing But Nets campaign is the world's largest grassroots effort working to save
lives and protect vulnerable families.

They identified a particular kind of donor in their database that they were hoping to replicate. In other words, they
wanted to find more people who fit the same profile. Could
we help them understand what these people cared about
and how to engage them and activate their help? Of course
we could! One of the things that drives us as a team is the
ability to use our data to help make the world a better place.

The donors they wanted to understand were medical

professionals who had donated to a global health care concern before and fit a specific list of other criteria. We recruited an Unlocking Survey respondent sample of 1,850 people who fit the description, and we were off to the races.

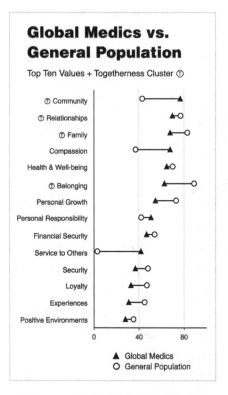

Global Medics vs. General Population

Top Ten Values + Togetherness Cluster ⑦

Like always, we asked our survey respondents a handful of questions to guide the extrapolation of data from our benchmark dataset. The chart I've included here is a super-duper broad overview that shows the shared values of the identified target audience compared to the general population of the United States.

This target audience is a unique subset of Americans for

many reasons, but one in particular stands out. *Community* ranks as the most important value in their lives.

I've never seen this before or since. *Community* is more important than *Family*, *Belonging*, or any of the other values that we are accustomed to ranking in the number-one spot. More than anything else, these donors will gravitate toward anything that helps them connect, protect, and improve the communities they care about most.

Think about how you could build a messaging platform around that one data point.

- How could you connect donors to a specific *Community* where their donation will have an impact?

- Can you use technology to allow donors to connect to each other and form *Community* among themselves?

- Could you foster a sense of *Community* by hosting meetups and events where donors can hear directly from individuals in the *Community* where their funds have been directed?

I'll close this case story with an open invitation to anyone reading this book. We're always on the lookout for global organizations who can use our global database to make good things happen. If that's you, reach out. We'd love to talk.

THE GORE-TEX WARS: NORTH FACE VERSUS PATAGONIA

It takes a lot to surprise me, but the valuegraphics from this study did. After years of profiling target audiences for companies all over the world, you think you've seen it all, and then you get a result like this.

For two companies that are in the same sector, competing for the same share of mind, I would have expected to see some nuanced differences—a molehill of variance, not a mountain—between their target audiences. But this? This is the Mount Kilimanjaro of differences. Let's break it down.

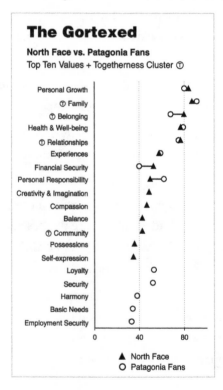

The Gortexed

North Face vs. Patagonia Fans
Top Ten Values + Togetherness Cluster ⓣ

Personal Growth	
ⓣ Family	
ⓣ Belonging	
Health & Well-being	
ⓣ Relationships	
Experiences	
Financial Security	
Personal Responsibility	
Creativity & Imagination	
Compassion	
Balance	
ⓣ Community	
Possessions	
Self-expression	
Loyalty	
Security	
Harmony	
Basic Needs	
Employment Security	

▲ North Face
○ Patagonia Fans

The North Face customer is driven by *Belonging* and a sense of *Community* that outstrips the Patagonia customer by a mile. Anecdotally, I see North Face logos all over the people working on movie sets here where I live in Vancouver, often referred to as Hollywood North, and so the importance of *Creativity* and *Self-Expression* shouldn't come as a surprise. It's rare to see *Balance* and *Compassion* in a consumer product profile like this, so that's worth noting. But before we end up convinced the North Face fan is some kind of misunderstood Zen mountain poet, note how much importance they place on *Financial Security* and *Possessions*. They want to maintain their economically enabled lifestyle, and they love having stuff.

What should North Face do with this? Well, messages of technical craftsmanship and material suitability seem to be the norm in the sector, so assuming they have those covered, they might want to find ways to soften the edges of the brand a bit.

A campaign featuring the unsung heroes of backcountry creativity? The Banff School of the Arts hosts the Mountain Film Festival every year, where the world's best films about mountain lifestyles are screened and trophies are handed out. A heavy-duty sponsorship of that event seems like it would be a natural fit. Particularly if there was a way to directly involve North Face customers around the world to boost *Belonging* and *Community*. How about a North Face livestreaming channel for all the movies screened at the festival in real time and digital front-row seats at the awards show, too? Could the winning filmmakers have a Zoom meet and greet with North Face customers?

Patagonia customers are an entirely different breed. They will gravitate to anything that can help them achieve more *Personal Responsibility*, a value we often see associated with environmentalism. They want to find ways to be the one who makes things happen. Add to that the importance they place on *Loyalty*, and these would be prime prospects for involvement in some sort of ongoing brand-sponsored activism that hinges on their own actions. Maybe there are micro-grants that Patagonia customers can apply for that could be used to help with small-scale change in a million neighborhoods around the planet, one initiative at a time.

The other distinguishing valuegraphic cluster for Patagonia customers includes *Security*, *Basic Needs,* and *Employment Security.* Compared to North Face fans, these folks want to feel wrapped up in a warm blanket of fiscal assurance. They think about how their actions will impact their jobs, their ability to pay the rent and put food on the table, and their safety in an increasingly volatile world.

If either brand wants to go on the offensive and look to steal share while simultaneously solidifying their base, the North Star to guide that activity is provided by the Valuegraphics Profile, too. The values shared by both target audiences, if amplified by either brand, would be the easiest way to have your freeze-dried backcountry-camping foil pouch of cake and eat it, too.

GLOSSARY OF TERMS

THE VALUEGRAPHICS PROJECT: We work to accomplish our vision of a values-driven post-demographic world in various ways, all of which are nestled under the umbrella of the Valuegraphics Project.

- **THE VALUEGRAPHICS DATABASE** is our proprietary benchmark dataset. As this book goes to press, the database includes responses from 750,000 surveys in a random, stratified, statistically representative sample of the population of nine regions of the world. It encompasses 180 countries, uses 152 languages, and measures the 56 core human values plus an additional 380 questions about wants, needs, and expectations, for a total of 436 metrics.

The data is +/–3.5% accurate with a 95% degree of confidence.

- **THE VALUEGRAPHICS RESEARCH COMPANY** provides organizations with valuegraphic target audience profiles and personas, using our proprietary methodologies and database. Projects can be global, regional, or microtargeted geographically (right down to the level of IP addresses).

- **THE VALUEGRAPHICS ACADEMY** focuses on outreach and education, conferences, events, online learning, certifications, and more.

- **THE VALUEGRAPHICS INSTITUTE** works with global not-for-profit organizations to advance their work by donating valuegraphic research and insights.

- **DAVID ALLISON INC.** is the home of my books and my work as a speaker.

VALUEGRAPHICS ARCHETYPE: For the custom research work we do with our clients, the Valuegraphics Database has the potential to yield untold hundreds of thousands of different target audience profiles, if not more. To make a DIY version that's workable within the confines of this book, we arranged the population of the world—very roughly—into 15 archetypes. These could be thought of as the biggest, broadest tribes on the planet.

VALUEGRAPHICS ARCHETYPE QUIZ: A quick-and-easy quiz designed to help organizations figure out which of the 15

Valuegraphics Archetypes apply to the target audience they are focused on.

SUPERHERO ARCHETYPE: The archetype that is most applicable to the target audience identified by the Valuegraphics Archetype Quiz.

SIDEKICK ARCHETYPE: A close runner-up to the Superhero Archetype, which may add a layer of nuanced understanding to the target audience in question.

NEMESIS ARCHETYPE: The archetype that is most *unlike* the target audience profiled by the Valuegraphics Archetype Quiz. Knowing what a target audience is *not* can sometimes be a valuable perspective.

VALUEGRAPHICS PROFILE: A general term that can be applied to a valuegraphic description of a target audience.

CUSTOM VALUEGRAPHICS PROFILE: The highly accurate and nuanced version of a Valuegraphics Profile that we create for our clients.

UNLOCKING SURVEY: When we are engaged in creating a Custom Valuegraphics Profile, the first step is to send an Unlocking Survey to a statistically representative sample of the target audience in question. Depending on several factors, these short surveys require a sample size of at least 1,350 participants who meet a series of qualifications. Based on the data collected, we unlock the benchmark dataset—the Valuegraphics Database—and extrapolate the Custom Valuegraphics Profiles.

VALUES THINKING: Like Design Thinking, Values Thinking is a simple process to tackle any issue or question that may arise. It enables organizations to keep the values of their target audience at the center of their solutions and strategies.

MAGNETIC VALUES: When solving any issue with valuegraphic insights at hand, a small selection of values will often be chosen as the most relevant to the situation. It's useful to refer to that small handful of values as the Magnetic Values, as they are the tools chosen to create the most magnetically powerful strategies.

HAVE YOU FLIPPED TO THE LAST PAGE WITHOUT READING THIS BOOK?

If you've flipped back here, it means you are at least *thinking* about reading this book, and that means you've given me the gift of your attention, even if just for a few minutes. Thank you for that! But I do understand how busy everyone is, so if you'd rather just watch a five-minute video synopsis of this book, you can find it at **www.valuegraphicsbook.com**.